ALMOST GOODBYE

HOW THE MOST BEAUTIFUL HORSE IN THE WORLD CHANGED MY LIFE

TAMMY WALDROP

Dirt Rhodes Publishing

Published by Dirt Rhodes Publishing

ISBN: 978-0-692-85845-5

Typesetting services by BOOKOW.COM

*For Johnny Pritchard, Matt Reynolds, Jason McClendon,
and all the other vets who sacrifice sleep, family time,
and more to help keep our beloved critters healthy*

Acknowledgments

Obviously, this book was a labor of love and I would like to thank some of the people who helped me along the way.

Julia Walker, author of an amazing memoir, *Fireball: The true story of a Tennessee plowgirl*, provided me with advice and wisdom, not only about the process of writing and publishing a book, but also about how to live with a little more grace and happiness.

The incredibly talented Janine Rhodes did a beautiful job of designing the book cover. She has come through for me many times and in many ways over the years. This is just the most recent of her rescue operations. And I'm sure it's not the last.

Thanks also to Steve Passiouras at bookow.com for his patience and professionalism.

My dear friends Camilla Herold, Melissa Hamilton, Heather May, and Sherry Wade all gave me excellent feedback and encouragement. I love them all and appreciate their help more than they'll ever know. To all my other friends, too numerous to mention, who have listened to my stories and put up with me over the years, thank you.

Margaret and Al Koger and Cassie Williamson were instrumental in bringing Aries into my life and for that the words "thank you" are inadequate.

My son Joey patiently read draft after draft of my manuscript and always offered honest opinions and advice. I would never have finished without his constant encouragement. He always pushes me to be more and do more and I am so proud of the man he has become. I also have to thank him for the hugs when I needed them most.

My oldest daughter requested that I change her name in the book, simply because she is a very private person, but this book is as much about her amazing strength and character as it is about Aries and me. God knew what he was doing when he made her my firstborn. I can't imagine how I'd have ever made it through life without her.

My Shannon, my special middle child, has always been my biggest cheerleader. She calls me "pretty" even when I'm not. She has taught me so much about kindness and patience and love. She has the biggest heart of anyone I've ever known. I am truly blessed by all three of my wonderful children, and I appreciate the tolerance they all gave me over my many mistakes and blunders, and the way they let me love Aries and knew that my affection for him did not in any way detract from the love I held for them.

And lastly of course, I have one final thank you for my beautiful Aries. He was the love of my life and I will never be the same without him. Until we meet again at the Rainbow Bridge, my friend.

CONTENTS

PROLOGUE

I slowed the car and turned off the headlights. I didn't want to wake anyone in the house, and the car was an exceedingly noisy one. The sound it made was so unique that co-workers always knew when I was arriving without even seeing me or my car.

I turned into the driveway and coasted between the two neat rows of wood fencing that lined the turnout paddocks at Rock House Ranch. There were no horses in the paddocks. They were all in the barn, dozing or munching on hay or whatever else horses do in the middle of the night.

I wasn't lucky enough for the gate to be open. Luck was not something that visited me often, so I wasn't surprised. I stopped, rolled my window down and reached out to open the car door. It didn't open from the inside. I stepped out, walking past the mangled front bumper of the car. My brother had first crushed it during an icy road incident, and I had since compounded the damage by striking a deer on my way home from work one night. Luck wasn't often with either of us.

I unlatched the gate, opened it, and got back in the car. I had to be very gentle on the accelerator, barely touching it with my ugly black skid-resistant shoe. I pulled through the gate, carefully scrutinizing the small, neat house at the end of the driveway. Good. No sign of lights. Everyone was sound asleep. That "everyone" included my oldest daughter Katie, who was thankfully safe in a warm bed with clean sheets tonight. Chris and Mona, the owners of the ranch, had welcomed her with open arms.

I pulled to the left and parked in front of the big red barn, so no one could see the car from the house. If someone got up to pee or get a drink of water in the wee hours of the morning, I didn't want them to see it there. I walked back and shut the gate, and then went toward the barn, choosing to walk around the back side of it, still afraid that someone would spot me, as if I were a commando conducting a midnight raid.

The horses, with their large, flexible ears, could definitely hear me, despite my pathetic attempt at stealth. Heads began poking out over stall doors, a row of different-colored faces in the moonlight, all facing me in puzzlement. Who was this crazy lady and what was she up to in the middle of the night? And most importantly, did she have apples? Or maybe peppermints?

I paused at one of the doors. My oldest daughter's first pony, Ebony, looked at me with calculating eyes, torn between flattening his ears against his head and pricking them forward. Ebony and I had a long and uneven history. He wasn't sure whether to hate me or ingratiate himself to me. I often did have apples, after all. Hence the indecisive ears.

But this night, I did not have apples. A fact he confirmed the second I reached an empty hand over his stall door to pat his neck. He jerked his head back inside his stall and turned his rump toward me. Perfect. Just how this night was going. *Don't have anything for me, lady? Then I've no use for you. Put out or get out.*

The next stall over, gentle Mr. Pibb looked at me with a more sympathetic face. Pibb belonged to my younger daughter Shannon. He was a sorrel and white pinto pony, with a slightly shaggy mane and a square muzzle. We called him the solid gold pony. I had trusted Pibb to carry Shannon through her Special Olympic competitions, through "regular" horse shows, and all over the place. He couldn't carry much of anything anymore, but he still exuded that sweet spirit. He let me pet him, even without apples, but then he too, turned away, toward a bit of hay that he had left over from dinner. Now that I'd woke him up, this was the perfect time to finish it.

Around the corner, right next to the wash rack, was the stall I was headed for. It faced the house, so it was risky, but it was worth it. This stall didn't open at the top so the horse could hang his head over. Instead, it had bars in the center of it and a drop-down latch with an extra snap hook on it. The occupant was a bit of an escape artist.

I flattened myself against the barn wall in my best spy-movie stance, difficult to pull off in my Shoney's uniform, which consisted of a pink shirt with an enormous butterfly-like bow tie under the chin and a black wrap-around skirt. When a toddler had exposed my backside to the entire restaurant one night by pulling on the edge of that stupid skirt, I had wanted to strangle whoever designed it, along with the person who decided that it would be perfect for waitresses to wear. Waitresses. Not waiters. Waiters got to wear pants, which never blew up in the wind or got pulled aside by grubby-handed toddlers. It was 1991, for crying out loud. It was ok for women to wear pants. But the restaurant business liked to dress their females differently than the males, a trend that was destined to continue. My wrap-around skirt was nothing compared to orange hot pants or mini-kilts.

I scoped out the yard between the barn and the house. Still no lights or signs of anybody stirring. The barnyard was well-lit, though, and if anyone was looking out a window, they'd definitely see me. I'd have to be quick.

I took a deep breath and went for it, fumbling for just a second with that extra snap hook. Then the door slid open quietly, and I stepped inside, sliding it shut behind me. I moved away from the stall door, so nobody in the house could spot the pastel pink of my shirt through the bars of the window. As if anyone in the house was on sentry duty, alert for waitresses invading the boarder's stalls.

For some reason, I flattened myself along the wall in the same spy-movie stance I'd adopted moments before. I just felt so guilty and paranoid, skulking around in the middle of the night. And yet, I didn't have anywhere else to go. I was homeless.

Homeless. The word seemed so harsh, although I'd never really had a place that *felt* like home. But to have nowhere to go, no one to turn to, no welcoming family members, no friends upon whose couch I could crash … it was a little overwhelming. I had visions of begging on a street corner, three months of dirt caked on my skin, never to see my kids or my critters again. "This is how it begins," I thought, and a familiar wave of panic swept over me, gripping my gut and making my hands tremble.

As my eyes adjusted to the darkness in the stall, I could see Aries, lying in the shavings, his legs tucked underneath him. While horses are capable of sleeping on their feet, and often do so, Aries preferred to sleep lying down, curled up like a dog on a pillow.

He blinked up at me sleepily and squinted, probably in the same manner that I was squinting at him. He rose to his feet, putting his forelegs in front of him and pushing off with his hind legs. Horses, those most graceful of all creatures on God's earth, aren't all that graceful in rising. Or quick. Which is probably why most horses sleep standing up, ready to flee from predators at a moment's notice.

But Aries wasn't concerned about predators. He was comfortable and safe in his stall. He rose and shook himself, bits of shavings flying off his beautiful grey form.

I was still plastered against the wall, my arms outstretched, my panic attack pinning me there like a moth on black velvet.

And Aries took a couple of steps forward, stopped, and dropped his head. He pressed his forehead against my chest. No questions. No judgments. No explanations or favors required. He was just happy to see me. Granted, he'd probably have been even happier if I'd had apples, but still...

It was a simple gesture, like a dog resting his chin on your knee, gazing up at you with adoration. Or a cat, curling up on your lap because they adore your warmth.

But I could feel the anxiety draining away as if the gentle pressure of Aries' head on my chest was pressing it out, tension just oozing out my fingers and toes. I peeled one arm off the wall and pulled a bit of hay out of Aries' forelock. Then I put my head down against his and I cried. But these were not tears of fear or anxiety, like most of the gajillions of tears I would shed during my life. These were tears of joy. Tears of relief. I was safe. I was happy. After the previous three nights of events, I thought those were two words that might never describe me again.

* * *

Our lives are filled with pivotal moments. Moments that change our perspective. Moments that change our way of thinking. Moments that change our life's direction. These moments are usually hard to identify while they're happening, because they aren't filled with a swell of motivational music, like in the movies. They are generally only identified through hindsight.

So that night, in that quiet, dark stall with no inspirational music, no glitter falling from the rafters, no spotlights shining on my tears, I didn't recognize the significance of the moment.

I had always admired Aries, mostly in secret and for a while, from afar. But that night, in the depths of desperation, that simple gesture changed me. It gave me hope. It gave me strength. It may sound melodramatic, but in retrospect I cannot overstate the impact that moment had on the rest of my life. Or on the bond it created between Aries and me.

* * *

I pulled Aries' blanket off his blanket bar and spread it out on the shavings. I wrapped myself in it, bunching up a bit of it to use as a pillow. And I fell asleep for the first time in more than 48 hours. I didn't have long before I'd have to get up and leave. Farm folk tend to be early risers, and I didn't want anyone to find me there. But I got a few glorious hours of sleep, although several times I woke up enough to steal a look at Aries.

He never laid back down, and he also didn't seem to sleep. Because every time I looked at him, he was watching me. But in my mind, he was watching *over* me.

1 THE FLYER

IT all began a few years earlier with a crumpled piece of paper in the bottom of my daughter's backpack. A piece of paper that so easily could have been thrown away, overlooked, or ignored. Obviously, I don't know how my life would have turned out had I not seen this piece of paper, but I am so grateful that I did.

* * *

I puttered into the parking lot and pulled to the yellow line that marked the spot where the parent's cars were supposed to start lining up. I shut the engine off and got out, leaning against the car while I waited anxiously for Shannon to appear. I was early. I was always early. I was perhaps a bit overly protective of Shannon.

Today, they have a term for mothers who worry too much about their kids. They're called "helicopter moms," because they hover around.

By those standards, I wasn't just a helicopter – I was Blackhawk. But I was a *stealth* Blackhawk. Oh, I had the machine guns and missiles, ready to annihilate anyone who messed with my child. But I'd rather not. I'd rather just fly under the radar and not expose her (or me) to anything that required me to break out those machine guns.

Some of my obsessive protectiveness was due to my own personality. I had what could be referred to as "social anxiety." Back in my day, they called people like me "painfully shy." It wasn't that I didn't like people. I was just terrified of them.

But there were other reasons.

* * *

One reason was a conversation with a therapist. The one who recommended "early intervention" for Shannon. My beautiful sweet child had been diagnosed as moderately mentally retarded. That word. The "R" word. How I despise that word. Want to activate my machine guns? Just say it in front of me.

Their recommendation for early intervention involved Shannon attending a training center. In those days the prevailing theory was that people like Shannon couldn't actually *learn*, but they could be trained. Like a dog. There was even a term for it. Trainably Mentally Retarded. TMR.

Even though Shannon was officially MMR, rather than TMR, the recommendation was still for her to attend a nearby training center. I visited the center, and it gave me an uneasy, queasy feeling in my stomach. It was dark and dank and smelled vaguely of urine and frozen pizza. And I'd never been away from Shannon, so the idea of handing her over to complete strangers in a building that smelled funny and made my stomach queasy was not a welcome one.

But they didn't give me an option. This wasn't really a recommendation. It was a mandate.

But I didn't get that at first. I thought I had a choice. I was her mother, after all. It shouldn't matter that they thought I wasn't really old enough to be her mother. I had run away from home at the oh-so-mature age of sixteen to get married, and had my first daughter at seventeen. Shannon came along a scant 14 months later. Marriage wasn't what I expected. I wasn't good at it. Motherhood, on the other hand ... that I was good at. Or at least I thought so.

I was sitting in a room, staring at the floor as usual, looking at the therapist's polished toes encased in chic and probably expensive high heels. I was barely out of my teens and had never even worn a pair of heels myself. My own shoes were dollar store sneakers with holes in the toes, slightly stained with Georgia red clay. I tried to tuck them self-consciously underneath my chair.

And I asked the therapist what would happen if I refused to take Shannon to this training center.

She paused and leaned down slightly to catch my eyes. She made sure she had eye contact with me ... hard eye contact, which made me squirm a bit before she even spoke. When she did speak, she spoke very slowly and enunciated her words very precisely. Careful. She was being Careful.

"If you refuse, the state could take custody of Shannon, to make sure that she gets appropriate care and intervention. She would be taken to the Georgia Mental Retardation Center, and you would not be allowed to see her. Do you understand what I'm saying?"

I was out of my league, sitting there in that austere examining room with my ragged jeans and stained sneakers, but I wasn't entirely stupid. I was, however, accustomed to being perceived as such. My obvious poverty combined with my southern-country-redneck accent made that a foregone conclusion for most people. I pushed down the ball of fury that was burning in my gut at the suggestion that anyone would be able to take my child from me. *Over my dead body* was the southern-country-redneck term fixed in my head. But I had to think. I had to be smart. This woman had power. This woman was dangerous. She was being careful. I had to be more careful. It was a mistake for me to use the word "refuse." I couldn't make another mistake like that. Because I had also been to the Georgia Retardation Center. And the queasy feeling I got when visiting the training center was nothing compared to the full-blown panic that engulfed me at the thought of Shannon being housed in that building.

So I formulated my response carefully. I couldn't go toe to toe with this woman. I couldn't argue. I had to roll over and show my soft underbelly. Or she would rip my throat out and take my child.

"I've just never been away from her." *Make this about your insecurity, not criticism for their system.* "Could we maybe start with a couple of days a week?" *Phrase it as a request. Be polite. Be ingratiating. Grovel if you have to.* "Maybe they could teach me what to do to help her at home." *Appeal to her ego. Negotiate.*

I watched her relax, her face soften, her shoulders lowering just a tad.

"We may be able to work something out. But we would need to do a home visit, to determine the best situation for Shannon and to teach you how to properly care for her."

"Thank you," I said. "That would be very helpful." *You vicious bitch. I hope you break your ankle in those stupid heels.*

Several years later, the Georgia Mental Retardation Center would be in the news, investigated for over 150 suspicious deaths over the years. It would be renamed when the "R" word began to finally fall out of favor … when it enraged parents with more clout and power than me. And it would close its doors forever sometime in the 1990s.

Shannon escaped the nightmare that was the Georgia Retardation Center, but she did attend the recommended training center for about a year, three days a week, until she was five and could go to a public kindergarten, attending a special education class.

* * *

And that's where I was that muggy September day, leaning against my car at Shannon's kindergarten, awaiting the appearance of my half-a-heart.

The second I saw her, my anxiety dissolved. She was so stinking cute in a dress I'd made her, her huge plastic-framed glasses giving her that sweet owlish look. A Scooby-Doo lunch box dangled from her hand and as soon as she saw me, she smiled, walking faster toward me. She knew not to run. Running was against the rules, and Shannon was a strict rule-follower.

On the drive home, I asked her about her day at school. I was always so worried about what happened to her during those long hours of separation. Did she get scared? Did the other kids bother her? Make fun of her? Did she get lost in the hallway, looking for the bathroom?

Shannon's verbal skills weren't the best and her voice was loud and a little harsh because of nodules she had on her vocal cords. I worried that talking made her throat sore, but had been assured that this was not the case. Still, she tended to answer questions with one or two words, and she almost never volunteered information, so I was unable to formulate a clear picture of her daily routine.

We pulled into the driveway of our little trailer in the woods. It was ancient and decrepit, with stained carpet and holes in the floor. We never had to let the cat out to use the bathroom. It just crawled in and out of the holes in the floor.

* * *

During the therapist-mandated home visit by the representatives of the Mental Health Division of the Department of Human Resources, I tried to cover up those holes with rugs and prayed the cat wouldn't pick that hour to wriggle in from outside, poking her snowy head out from under one of the rugs. I needn't have worried. The cat never saw people other than us and she wasn't about to enter that trailer with strangers inside. And the placement of the rugs may have puzzled the three people who visited me, but they didn't mention them or attempt to look under them. That was about the only thing they didn't look under, however.

They went into each room, opened every drawer, every cabinet door. Were they looking for drugs? I didn't even drink alcohol at the time, and wouldn't allow my husband to so much as bring a beer into the house. I was raised a Quaker, after all. But I supposed they didn't know that. I supposed they were looking out for Shannon's best interests.

They asked me hundreds of questions, which I answered awkwardly, my panic building by the minute. I was so sure they were going to find my home inadequate. My care of Shannon inadequate. Me inadequate. What would I do then? Would they attempt to take her that very day? Wrest her from my arms and carry her away? I wondered if they'd brought guns with them. Because I thought that was the only way they'd get her away from me.

In the end, I think it was my refrigerator that tipped the scales in my favor. Not its contents, although they definitely checked that out. But the front of the refrigerator, where I had stuck photos and drawings the girls had made. I thought that was something all mothers did, but apparently not, as one of my visitors explained to me. She said it indicated that I cared about my children. That they were a priority. Then she told me that they thought the best place for Shannon was with me ... as long as I agreed to let her attend the training center, where they could keep an eye on her progress.

I was deeply relieved when that visit was over, but the experience left me with an abiding fear of losing my children, and increased my social anxiety. As a result, we rarely left our little trailer, and other than school, the girls were almost never out of my sight.

* * *

Shannon dropped her backpack in the floor the moment she entered the door and went to turn on the television to watch afternoon cartoons.

I picked up her backpack. It often contained clues about how her day had been, so I always went through it as soon as we got home. There were never graded tests and books like her older sister brought home, but sometimes informative notes from her teacher. On this particular day, there wasn't much to find in her backpack, but I did pull out a crumpled sheet of paper. It was an invitation to attend a therapeutic horseback riding program for the handicapped. They had classes every Saturday morning.

"Shannon!" I said, feeling more excited than I had about anything in a long time. "Would you like to go ride a horse?"

She didn't answer me, her eyes glued to the television.

My feelings about animals were pretty much the opposite of my feelings about people. I was drawn to them, and I was especially drawn to horses.

I grew up dreaming about horses – riding in the back seat of the car, I would stare out the window, just hoping for a fleeting glimpse of one of those magical creatures. I read every horse book I could get my hands on, and one of the highlights of my life had been meeting Marguerite Henry, the author of *Misty of Chincoteague* and other children's books about horses.

So Shannon's lack of enthusiasm didn't dampen my excitement at all. Her sister would be home soon, and I knew she would share my excitement, because she shared my love of horses. I read the flyer again carefully, looking for anything that suggested we would have to pay for riding the horses, but it seemed as if it was totally free. No catches. I was thrilled, because money was always in short supply.

I walked into the kitchen and looked at my refrigerator. That jumble of photos and drawings had helped keep my Shannon with me, so my refrigerator door had become a shrine to me. I pulled a magnet off and slid the flyer underneath, smoothing out the crumpled edges. Then I went back into the living room, to sit beside Shannon in the floor until her sister came home.

2 KAREN HILL ACADEMY

THE following Saturday morning, the girls and I left our little trailer in the woods and set off on our life-changing adventure.

It was a chilly autumn morning, probably the first one of the season – that day when you walk out onto your porch expecting to feel the usual Georgia heat, and instead go back inside to grab a jacket or sweater. In other words, the best day of the year in the South.

The drive was leisurely and scenic. Georgia may not offer the same spectacular fall colors as I've heard you find in New England, but the dogwoods offered up crimson to purple, and the abundant peach and pecan trees mixed in more shades of gold and red. The car was quiet, as it often was. My girls weren't your stereotypical chatterboxes.

Karen Hill Riding Academy for the Handicapped was located just outside tiny Palmetto, Georgia, on the property that was once home to a racetrack called Holiday Downs.

When we pulled in, we saw a dilapidated barn ahead of us, but what caught our attention was a flashing herd of horses on the right side of the long driveway. They were trotting around with lovely floating trots and tossing their heads in an odd way that I would come to know and love as uniquely Arabian.

They were mostly older mares in varying shades of grey and chestnut. The one that attracted my attention however, was a gangly dappled grey gelding. Even my inexperienced eye could detect his rank in that frolicking herd. He was the exuberant teenager. The one that sometimes irked the mares with his antics and curiosity, but they tolerated him and loved him. That didn't mean he didn't see the business end of their heels or teeth from time to time. They had to keep him in line and raise him up right, after all.

As we pulled further down the driveway, I tore my eyes away from the show the horses were putting on, and saw a group of people gathered in front of the barn. As we stepped out, we were greeted by a smiling woman with short-cropped silver hair, wearing a grey sweatshirt.

"Welcome!" she said as she drew near. "I'm Margaret Koger. Tell me about your child's disability."

I was startled by her direct inquiry. There was no preamble, no tiptoeing around the subject, no hinting around. The only places I had experienced that kind of matter-of-fact treatment was in a medical or school setting.

So Margaret's innocent and sincere welcome felt to me like being locked in a dark room, when suddenly a smiling torture expert shines a 1000 watt flashlight directly into your eyes and demands cheerily that you name *it*. Say out loud that thing that stole away your precious child's chance at a "normal" life. Name that thing that dashed to tiny, irretrievable pieces your hopes and dreams for her future. Give *it* a name – that thing that was threatening her physical health and perhaps even her life. Say it in front of her and say it with a smile.

It crossed my mind to get back in the car and leave. Bank my Blackhawk to the right and fly to the safety of our trailer in the woods. But there were those horses, still visible in the corner of my eye, a tantalizing dance of beauty and peace ...

So I fought the rising flush in my cheeks and introduced Shannon, with a deliberately vague explanation of Shannon's official diagnosis.

After establishing Shannon's limitations, we were introduced to the rest of the group and filled in on their "problems" as well ... though none of them seemed bothered or inhibited by their differences at all.

There was Emilie, a short, stout woman with Down's Syndrome, and her parents, George and Rebecca. Sweet Denise had cerebral palsy, and was in attendance every Saturday morning with her grandmother, Miss

Betty, who was raising her. Robbie was a handsome teenager in a wheel-chair, and Anne was a middle-aged woman with Tourette's. I had never heard of Tourette's at the time, so Anne's frequent expletives were un-settling at first, but her demeanor otherwise was pleasant. We just over-looked the occasional "fuck you" and didn't take it personally. There were others who came once in a while, but we quickly learned that this was the core group – the ones who showed up without fail every week.

The volunteers were about the same. Sometimes, a group would show up from 4-H or to get volunteer credit for a class or project, but the faithful ones were a small, tightly knit group. There was Tammie, a red-haired teenager, upon whom Robbie had an obvious crush. There was Brenda, a blond British lady, who brought her daughter Victoria to help out and to be close to the horses. And then there were the Bryant sisters. Cassie was the main volunteer at the Academy. She lived nearby and she and her siblings were all home-schooled, so she was able to help take care of the horses on a daily basis, not just on weekends. Cassie's younger sister Emily helped out as well but there was no denying Cassie's influence on everything at Karen Hill.

That first day, Shannon rode a horse named Stanley. He was a rangy thoroughbred-cross with stockings and a blaze. Some participants rode the same horse every week, and developed a close relationship to them. Emilie always rode Lady, who was a dark bay with a thick neck and a roached mane. Her breed was uncertain, like most of the school horses, but she was short and stout, like Emilie. Happy-go-lucky Denise usu-ally rode an elderly palomino named Katie. Once we became regulars at Karen Hill, Katie would become known as "Katie the horse," to differ-entiate her from my daughter Katie.

My Katie took to Cassie like a magnet, following her around and lis-tening to everything she had to say. Cassie had Shannon help her groom and tack up Stanley. Taking care of the horses was an important aspect of the therapy, equal in importance to the actual riding. It was beneficial for riders, who were used to people taking care of them, to be responsible for the care of another creature. It also fostered the emotional bond between them and the horse.

As soon as the horses were tacked up, they were taken to a small riding ring, to be led around by volunteers. A few of the more experienced riders were capable of handling the horse on their own, but most had a leader, and all had a walker beside them, in case anything went awry.

There was a ramp for Robbie, to wheel up to back-level of the horse, and then several volunteers helped lower him into the saddle. The school horses were marvels of patience and tolerance, standing quietly to allow the safe transfer of their cargo.

Margaret allowed Katie to lead her sister's horse during that first lesson. Shannon was utterly fearless, trusting her sister and Stanley completely. They only walked around in circles for about 30 minutes, while Cassie stood in the center of the ring and gave some basic instructions – heels down, back straight, good job!

Katie helped Shannon untack Stanley and together, they brushed him off. Then, with Cassie supervising, they led him to the pasture and took his halter off, leaving him free to roll in the grass and enjoy the rest of that beautiful Saturday.

We had just gotten in the car to leave, when Margaret waved at me to wait. She walked over to the car as I rolled my window down. She said that the volunteers often rode themselves after lessons were over, and Cassie was wondering if Katie would like to stay and ride with them.

I knew the answer to that question without even turning my head to see those eager blue eyes pleading with me. So I turned the ignition off and we all got out again.

Katie was much younger than the rest of the volunteers. They were mostly teenagers, like Cassie. I knew it was very kind of them to include the new kid in their weekly ride, and I was grateful for it.

Katie rode a spotted pony named Stormy that day. Stormy was a POA, a "Pony of the Americas." It was a breed I had never heard of, so Margaret gave me a brief history while we waited for the girls to finish their ride.

The breed was a cross between Arabs, Appaloosas, and Shetlands. They were like miniature, elegant Appaloosas. They had only been around since the 1950s, so there still weren't very many of them, perhaps only about 2,000. Stormy was in his golden years, having carried Margaret's daughters through countless horse shows and trail rides. Katie looked right at home atop Stormy, her strawberry blond hair streaming out from underneath her riding helmet, and her freckled face lit up with a blissful smile. It looked as if she'd found her place in the world.

On the ride home that day, Katie chattered non-stop about the horses, about Cassie, about all the nice people we'd met, and everything she'd learned. Shannon chimed in from time to time as well. I think my car was noisier than it had ever been. But I was quiet, dreaming about a gangly grey Arabian.

3 EPIPHANY

THE rumpled note hung on my refrigerator shrine for weeks. Maybe months. I didn't know the scope of its significance at the time, but I already knew that it had changed my life, and my children's lives, for the better.

Suddenly, we weren't shut-ins any more – captives to social anxiety and overprotectiveness and poverty.

Karen Hill Academy was designed to help the handicapped, but often, the real benefactors were the parents and siblings. That was certainly true in our case. While Shannon enjoyed the riding lessons, her sister reveled in them, soaking up information like a sponge, eager to help out and learn as much as she could about horses. And I was enticed out of the dark safety of our little trailer, forced to interact with humans in order to enjoy the company of the horses and to see my girls having so much fun.

During Shannon's diagnosis process, which involved several months of testing and numerous trips to the Children's Hospital in Atlanta, the doctors tried to give me some idea of what to expect for Shannon's future. I was told that, for example, she would probably never learn how to read. She could be taught to dress herself, they said. To brush her teeth and put her shoes on. But trying to teach her to read would be a waste of time.

As a lifelong lover of books, I found that notion unacceptable. And so I was determined to teach her to read. And I found that, while Shannon's reasoning skills and motor skills were lacking, her memory was nothing short of astounding.

And so we spent hours memorizing words. And trying to make those words meaningful to her. I got help in that endeavor from none other than the Atlanta Braves.

Shannon was fascinated by the Braves. She knew all the players. All the stats. Who was on the disabled list. Who was being traded. What the win/loss record was. All from watching television.

But she could get even more information from the newspaper. And so I used the newspaper to help her learn to read. We would pore over the sports section, reading not only about the Braves, but also about the University of Georgia Bulldogs, and all the local high school teams.

Because of all the time I put in, trying to help Shannon learn to read and to reach other developmental milestones that came so naturally to most children, I worried that I didn't give Katie as much attention as she needed. Katie was always very self-sufficient and understanding about Shannon's needs. She never demanded my time or seemed jealous that I gave more of it to Shannon.

And because we lived in the country, there were no neighborhood kids for Katie to play with. Just one girl about her age lived nearby. And although Katie and Shannon were just over a year apart in age, the gap in abilities kept them from playing together and interacting in the same way most siblings that close would.

Our time at Karen Hill gave us a focus, something the girls and I could enjoy together. We looked forward to Saturday mornings in the fresh air, and Shannon's motor skills improved by leaps and bounds. In fact, riding improved her balance and coordination much more than all the exercises the therapists had prescribed.

Most of the horses at Karen Hill were long past their prime, donated for a tax write-off by owners who didn't wish to care for a horse that was no longer useful. Ending up at Karen Hill or another therapeutic program was actually a best-case scenario for many of these horses, much preferable to the more final and traumatic options. This fact made me love those beautiful creatures even more. They were castaways, like me.

Margaret Koger struggled to keep the Academy afloat financially, partly because she couldn't seem to say "no" to any horse. The school horses were a small percentage of the horses that resided at Karen Hill. There were many others that had been donated because they had health or behavioral problems that made them unsuitable for any rider, much less a disabled rider.

Margaret's plan for these horses was to allow the volunteers to retrain or rehab them, and then sell them to make money to continue feeding the school horses. This sometimes worked out, but more often it seemed to me that it did not. Still, I admired her determination to give the horses a second chance. Sometimes, all one needs is a second chance.

Then there were the other equine residents of Karen Hill – Margaret and Al Koger's personal herd of Arabians. They were the horses we saw when we pulled in the driveway that first morning. They were mostly broodmares, and the young gelding that had caught my eye was out of Margaret's favorite mare. His barn name was Aries, for the astrological sign under which he was born. Many registered horses don't go by their registered name. Sometimes those names are long and hard to pronounce. Sometimes, a more suitable name just assigns itself to a particular horse due to personality quirks or physical attributes. So a horse will often have several names during its life. A registered name, a barn name, a show name ... and of course, if it changes owners, it can get a whole list of new names.

Aries' registered name was Ibn Alex. His sire's name was Alexander Spa Bask, and in Arabic, "ibn" means "son of." "Bint" means "daughter of" in Arabic, so in Arabian names, there tend to be a lot of "Bints" and "Ibns."

Aries was Cassie's pet project at Karen Hill. She was training him under saddle, with the hope of making a hunter/jumper out of him. Starting a horse under saddle is a huge responsibility. Whether the trainer is aware of it or not, that initial experience will affect the horse for better or worse, for its entire life.

While I admired Aries, however, another sort of animal had captured Katie's attention. His name was Ebony. Ebony was a large black pony of uncertain breed. He was not used in the riding program because he had an unacceptable habit. He liked to pull free from the person who was leading him and take off running for parts unknown. It didn't seem to matter to Ebony where he was going. He just enjoyed escaping from the human on the end of the lead.

The most common practice with a horse that has this inclination is to use a lead line that has a chain on the end of it. You run the chain through the ring on one side of the halter, run it over the horse's nose, through the ring on the other side, and fasten it underneath. It is the horsey equivalent of a dog's choke collar. The idea is that when the horse tries to break free, the chain tightens down on his muzzle, causing him discomfort and giving the human a little more control over a beast that outweighs them by several hundred pounds.

That strategy worked on Ebony ... sometimes. He was a very clever pony, and was extremely adept at reading that human on the end of the lead. Because those humans were often young volunteers with little or no real horse handling experience, Ebony could watch them and pick his moment to break free with little, if any, discomfort to his tender muzzle. Every time he got away with that trick, it became more engrained into his behavior and harder for anyone in the future to correct.

But there was not much Katie loved more than a good challenge. She was in mad-crazy-little-girl-horsey-love with a demon pony and nothing was going to keep her from acquiring him.

* * *

A couple years before, Katie had a birthday party, and lots of family members came. Several of them gave her five or ten dollars in a card, and when everyone left and we were cleaning up the kitchen, she counted her cash. She had thirty-five dollars.

"What should I buy with my birthday money?" she asked me.

"Well," I said, "What's something you really wanted for your birthday, but didn't get?"

"A horse," she replied. "But you can't buy a horse with $35." Her shoulders sagged as she considered the prospect of never having the thing she wanted most.

My mother's heart ached for her, because we mothers want our kids to have those things they want. Especially when we've experienced that same want ourselves and come out of it empty-handed.

"No, you can't buy a horse with $35," I said. "But if you save that $35 and add to it, eventually, you will have enough money to buy a horse."

Katie still wasn't convinced. She wanted to know how she was going to get more money. I told her that she could do odd jobs for her father and me. Her grandparents would probably help as well. And she could always save birthday and Christmas money. Still she was glum.

"But by the time I save enough money for a horse, I'll be a *teenager*."

I smiled, knowing how long that time span to her teen years seemed to her, and how rapidly it was going to fly by for me.

"So?" I said. "So you'll have a horse when you're a teenager. It's better than never having a horse at all, right?"

Standing in that shabby mobile home kitchen, I witnessed my just-turned-six daughter have an epiphany. Her shoulders squared and her expression changed and there was a determined light shining in her eyes. It gave me chills.

4 EBONY

KATIE's birthday epiphany had instilled in her an admirable work ethic that people still comment upon today. She would clean out her father's truck ... for a dollar. She would shine her grandfather's shoes ... for a dollar. She would fold the laundry and put it away for me ... for a dollar. Her bank contents added up more quickly the harder she worked, and she could see her goal becoming a reality. She saved pennies and nickels that nobody wanted.

So when she fell in love with Ebony, she already had some money saved up. She quickly struck a deal with Margaret Koger to buy her dream pony for a mere $500. But that's a lot of money when you're saving it a dollar and even a nickel at a time.

So by the time the deal was complete, some things had changed in our lives. The biggest change was probably her little brother. Little was a relative term, as "little" Joey was more than ten pounds and two feet long when he was born. I had struggled to lose weight after the girls were born, but my pregnancy with Joey took my weight to new dimensions. It was a little baffling to me, as I spent most of the pregnancy throwing up whatever food I was able to choke down. And afterward, with my weight at close to three hundred pounds, my social anxiety increased. I was always nervous, insecure, self-conscious of my appearance, and of people's reaction to me and to Shannon. And now Joey's obvious size (and mine) drew people's attention even more. People were always looking at us, always asking questions. For someone whose biggest wish in life was to simply be invisible, I was most definitely visible. We were hard to miss.

But rather than becoming the recluse I longed to be, I was spending even more time in public, because of the horses and the girls.

Our horsey time commitment had already grown from our once-a-week visit to Karen Hill to also include once-a-week riding lessons for Katie at an eventing farm in Newnan. Eventing consists of three separate competitions. On the lower levels, all three competitions are completed the same day, but on the more advanced levels, the competitions usually take place over three days ... dressage on the first day, show jumping on the second, and cross country on the third.

Katie had already competed in her first event, at Wood 'n Horse Farm, where she took lessons. Margaret loaned her Stormy, and they won a blue ribbon. At that point, it was all over but the shoutin', because Katie was hooked. She knew what she wanted to do with the rest of her life. But in order to advance, she needed to ride every day, and she needed her own horse to compete with. That was where Ebony came in.

And when the deal was finalized, that slender little red-head dragged a pillow case full of coins into the bank to turn them into paper money. She wanted to do it by herself, so I waited in the car. I'm sure the teller who had to count all those coins was not exactly thrilled by the task, but hopefully she was also impressed by Katie's single-minded determination.

But the purchase price of a horse or pony is the least of the expenses associated with equine ownership. They need food, shelter and medical care, just like humans. The first order of business was finding a place for Ebony to live. We wanted it to be nearby, because Katie didn't want to be too far away from her new love. Luckily, the area we lived in had numerous boarding facilities nearby. We decided on one in nearby Senoia.

Bar M Stables offered full, partial, or pasture board. Full board was the most expensive option but they would provide all feed, hay, and care for your horse. The horse received high-quality care with no time or effort required from the owners. No 6 a.m. feeding chores, no turn-out duty and definitely no stall mucking. Most people who went for this option were professionals with more money than time. They would typically show up once a week or once a month to enjoy a trail ride.

Pasture board was the least expensive option. Your horse was just turned out in the "back pasture," which had a lake for water and plenty of grass for food. Those owners also typically turned up only occasionally.

Partial board was the middle option financially. Your horse got a stall in the barn and you provided your own feed and hay. You fed your horse, you turned it out, and you cleaned its stall. We went for partial board for Ebony, which meant that we were at the barn every day, twice a day. At least.

We had only been at Bar M a week when we got schooled in what can happen when inexperienced people get in over their heads with horses. By this time, I thought I knew a lot about horses. That is when you are in the most danger, when you start to *think* you know what you're doing.

It had rained, and at Bar M, one of the rules for the partial-board pasture was that you didn't turn out your horses in the rain. It had only recently been reseeded and the horses would tear up the tender, relatively new grass when it was softened by rain. So Ebony, who was used to being out in a pasture most of the time, was suddenly confined to a stall for several days in a row.

By the time the sun came out and it was ok to turn them out, Ebony was chock full of pent-up energy and impatience to get out and run it off. He was so full of it that my normally fearless daughter was afraid to lead him to the pasture. So I did it.

I took the lead and threaded the chain over his nose, but still I had the distinct impression that Ebony was going to try and pull something. So I also held onto the side of his halter with my other hand, thinking that it gave me more control. I had heard the rule that you should never lead a horse by its halter, but I didn't fully understand the reason behind the rule. Ebony was about to give me a painful education.

We were about halfway to the pasture gate when it happened. Ebony had been quivering with anticipation and energy from the moment he stepped out of the stall, and he couldn't stand it anymore. He just HAD to run.

I could feel him bunching his muscles up, getting ready to run, so I gave him a little tug on the halter, just to let him know I was aware and alert. Alertness didn't help. He jerked his head away from me in response to my "warning" tug, which effectively pinned my hand between his face and the halter. Then he dug his powerful pony hindquarters in and went from his impatient prancing walk to a flat out run.

Ebony was large for a pony, but probably weighed between five and six hundred pounds. If it hadn't been so terrifying, I would have been extremely impressed at the ease with which that pony lifted me off my feet. With my hand caught in his halter, I was flapping along beside him like a scarf whipping in the wind for several strides. Then my hand came loose and I crashed to the ground.

It all happened so quickly, I was stunned, lying in the mud beside the manure pile. Katie came running up, asked if I was ok, and I told her I was fine. "Just get him!" I said.

Another boarder had witnessed the entire debacle, and helped Katie catch Ebony. She also used the chain on him, but she did it the proper way, and was able to get Ebony into the pasture for us.

As Katie and I were walking together toward the barn, I told her, "Katie, my arm is broken."

For some reason, she thought I was joking, and she laughed. But it was no joke. The other boarder asked me what was wrong, and I told her my arm was broken. It wasn't my first broken bone, and I wasn't speculating. I knew it was broken. But the boarder asked me if I could wiggle my fingers. I could, so she waved it away, saying it was fine. Not broken.

The x-rays disagreed with the barnyard diagnosis. I had broken both bones in my arm, the ulna and the radius, and for good measure had broken four or five of the eight bones in my wrist. I say four or five, because the doctor and the radiologist disagreed. The radiologist said five, but the doctor said he thought the fifth one was an old break that had healed.

I was awake for the surgery, and for some reason, it really distressed me that the surgeon used a Black and Decker drill to drive the pin into my arm. It seemed like it should be, well, surgical steel, and maybe have a medical company logo on it. Black and Decker seemed like a tool that should be used on a construction site, not an operating room. And it wasn't even a high-end construction tool. I remember thinking, "At least they could use a Mikita."

The surgeon had to put all his weight into that drill to get the pin to go in, and he commented that I had the hardest bones he'd ever seen. Coming from an orthopedic surgeon, I thought that was pretty cool, and gave thanks to my Grandma Great's milk cows and all the whole, fresh, unpasteurized milk I had drunk as a kid. Although, on the other hand, I have had way too many broken bones in my life, but at least it's not because my bones are inadequate. Just my lifestyle … and perhaps my judgment.

5 ELVIS

THE reporter wanted to talk to me. She held the microphone in her hand and smiled a practiced smile, standing too close, being too friendly. I shook inside. I didn't like talking to strangers at all, much less a bunch of high-falutin' strangers in nice clothes, and certainly not in front of a camera.

But Karen Hill Academy was in danger. The property had been sold and the New Owner had Big Plans that did not include housing a riding program for the handicapped.

Margaret Koger was doing her best to fight it. She was the one who had invited the reporters here, to see what happened at Karen Hill Academy. To show them what a difference that place, those horses, those people, were making in our lives. I just wanted to go on with our Saturday morning lessons, to chat with Miss Betty, and see Denise's big sincere smile and perfect happiness. To see newcomers be startled by Anne's innocent "fuck you" introductions. To sit with George and Rebecca and listen to Emilie chastise Lady and to watch Cassie and Katie work their magic with the horses and the kids. Watch them become more relaxed, more agile, more outgoing. Watch Shannon grow more confident and healthier week by week.

And so I sucked it up. If I could calm my trembling down and try to explain it all, try to convince the reporter and the public that this was a sacred place, this scrap of ground with the dilapidated barn and the castaway horses and the leftover people. That this was Important. More important than the money the New Owner planned to make by developing this property. The words to a song kept running through my head. *They paved paradise and put up a parking lot. Sha-na-na-na.*

And so I let them turn the camera my direction and film me in my bulky sweater and scraggly hair and thick glasses, so self-conscious of my appearance and stumbling over my words. I tried to explain what Karen Hill had meant to me and my girls. I failed miserably. In fact, the entire thing failed.

Because the New Owner didn't care what the public thought of him. He was going to develop this land and put in a subdivision with an air strip so rich folks with their own airplanes could have their shiny flying machines right in their backyards.

Everyone searched desperately for a new home, but finding a place large enough to accommodate all of the program's horses was a difficult job. They were split up and housed in temporary homes across several counties. The Kogers tried to keep Lady, Katie the horse, and Stormy together for as long as possible, to try to keep the program going.

I had no idea where most of the horses went, and had resigned myself to the thought that I was never going to see Aries again. I was surprised at how much distress his absence caused me. After all, I usually only saw him from afar, only occasionally being lucky enough to be present while Cassie was riding him, at which time I could get close enough to pat his gorgeous neck. No one else knew that it was any different from patting any of the other horses on the neck, but for me, it was a unique thrill. I was like that screaming girl on the front row of an Elvis concert who managed to touch the hem of his pants, awestruck and privileged by the experience.

We continued having lessons for a while, but at a different location almost every week. It grew difficult for many of the regulars to find the new locations and often the new places were much farther away than Holiday Downs. We all tried, but Karen Hill was falling apart.

And then we received even worse news. Margaret Koger had suffered a major stroke. The stress was just too much for her. Her husband Al took over and tried to keep the program afloat, but he was caring for an invalid wife, trying to remodel their condo to accommodate her wheelchair ... it was too much.

Finally, the calls went around to the dwindling Karen Hill faithful. It was over. No more lessons. I found it incredibly sad and ironic that Margaret, who had provided therapy for so many disabled people, was now disabled herself, and there was no equine therapy available to her. Her beloved horses were scattered and she would probably never see most of them again.

As sorry as I felt for Margaret, I felt a keen sense of loss myself. I had grown attached to the people and the horses at Karen Hill, and my Saturday mornings were not the same. And I missed Aries.

And then one day, my phone rang. I picked it up and heard a voice that was vaguely familiar, but I couldn't place it.

"Who?" I asked.

"Al Koger. Margaret's husband. From Karen Hill."

"Oh yes, Al. I'm so sorry. Didn't recognize your voice," I said. "How's Margaret doing?"

"She's getting a little better. Still not getting around, but talking more. We've been talking about you, actually."

"Me?" I was puzzled.

"Well, you and Katie. How's your arm doing?"

"Oh, it's fine," I replied. My arm had healed up so well, I almost forgot that I'd ever broken it sometimes.

"You know, I always felt bad about that," he said.

"Why?"

"Well, we knew you were new to horses. We should never have sold you that pony. We had other horses that would have been much more suitable."

I thought that he must not know Katie very well, because once she'd set her mind to getting Ebony, there was no changing her mind or convincing her to settle for anything "more suitable."

"It's been a learning experience for sure. But Ebony's doing great. Katie's been taking him to a lot of horse shows and they win quite a bit."

"That's kind of what I wanted to talk to you about."

I felt a stab of worry. Did he think we weren't taking good care of Ebony? I had been so embarrassed to reveal to them the reason for my broken arm. I remembered distinctly the look that had passed between Al and Margaret when I'd shown up that morning with my arm in a cast.

"We argued over it, Margaret and I. I thought it was irresponsible for us to sell you that pony. I just knew someone would get hurt. But she thought that you and Katie could turn him around."

"We have! He's doing great! And my arm was all my fault. Not his."

"Well, it was somewhat his fault. But I have to say, I'm impressed with you guys for sticking with it, and not giving up on him. That Katie is something else. She has a lot of potential. But she's not going to go anywhere with Ebony."

I was confused and slightly offended. I wasn't sure where this conversation was going. First he said that he was impressed with Katie, but then he said that she wasn't going anywhere. I didn't know what to say, so I remained silent as he continued.

"You know, I've had to find homes for all of our horses and the lesson horses. I've sold quite a few and found homes for others. I just have one left that I need to take care of. Aries. You know, the one that Cassie was training?"

I knew. My heart had leapt at the mere mention of his name. "Yes, I remember him."

"You know his dam was Fate, Margaret's favorite mare, so she's particularly fond of him."

I remembered Margaret telling me a story about the night Aries was born. She said there was a terrible thunderstorm and Fate did not come up to the barn to be fed. She had to go out looking for her with a flashlight and found her and her foal, soaked and shivering. I could imagine her gathering up the tiny wet foal and carrying it to the barn. That would have created a special bond, I'm sure.

"So Margaret and I were discussing it, and we want Katie to have Aries. She needs a bigger horse and a better quality horse if she's going to move up."

Now my heart was hammering so hard and fast, I could barely breathe. But it sank almost immediately. There was no way we could afford to buy Aries. I almost choked as I told Al we couldn't do it.

"You don't understand," he replied. "We want to give Aries to you. Margaret and I want him to have a good home. We know you'll take good care of him."

I couldn't say "yes" fast enough. I was touched and honored to think that they trusted us to take care of Aries. I was also thrilled that Katie would have a new horse. And my inner teenage fangirl was doing cartwheels inside. Elvis was moving in.

* * *

Katie and I were waiting in front of the barn the day he was supposed to arrive. We had arranged to have another stall next to Ebony, and it was already bedded with pine shavings and we had put fresh hay and water in it. Now we were just standing, with our eyes fixed on the driveway, waiting for the top of a horse trailer to appear and change our lives.

David Barnett, the manager of Bar M, was hanging around as well. David was a compact man with wiry white hair and a moustache. He typically rode racking horses, and had a big black Tennessee Walker stallion that was also named Ebony. David was loud and outspoken and had been working with horses probably all his life.

Finally, the trailer pulled down the driveway, and we watched as Cassie backed Aries out. He was much lighter in color than I had remembered, now a very light grey, almost white with just a few steel-grey dapples covering his hindquarters. He was perhaps a little thin but he had added muscle since I last saw him. His chest had grown wider and deeper, and his neck had begun to show a more muscular arch to it. But the most striking aspect of Aries' appearance was simply the way he carried himself, with an air of quiet elegance. I was overcome with emotion and admiration.

As Cassie handed over the lead rope to Katie, I heard David's exaggerated shocked exclamation from the barn behind us as he took the cigar out of his mouth. "He's an A-rab! You got an A-rab for that little girl? Don't you know all A-rabs are crazy?"

Al Koger was one of the mildest mannered men I have ever known, but he shot David a look, and I knew he was more than a little disturbed by the comments. David, of course, was oblivious and kept it up.

"You already had a broken arm. What are you trying to do, get your neck broke, too?" David laughed and I laughed too, but a tiny knot of apprehension grew in my stomach. David had a lot more experience than I did with horses. What if he was right, and we had bitten off more than we could chew? I really didn't know anything about Aries. Katie had never even ridden him. What if Katie was the one who got hurt this time?

Cassie and Katie were chattering excitedly and didn't even seem to notice what David was saying. Cassie was giving Katie lots of instructions, and I was trying to listen as well. I wanted to make sure Aries got the best care he'd ever had.

I tried to tune David out and talked with Al for a few moments while the girls introduced Aries to his new surroundings, walking him around and letting him take everything in.

"Don't listen to that guy," Al said. "We've owned Arabians for years. They're absolutely wonderful horses. They're just too intelligent for people like him to understand." He shot another dirty look in David's direction.

David kept up a steady stream of good-natured heckling in Aries' direction. It didn't seem to bother Katie in the least, and it certainly wasn't bothering Aries.

In the coming years, I would learn that people exhibit breed prejudice just like they do any other type of bias. Everyone believes that "their" breed is the best, which of course makes sense. That's why they chose that breed to begin with.

And Aries certainly didn't act crazy. Even though he was in a new place, and clearly curious about everything, he was perfectly well-behaved, following along behind Katie, while still scoping out his new environment.

And while David's banter was making me a little nervous, pretty much everything made me nervous, so it was okay.

6 MR. PIBB

SHANNON never asked for a horse. She seemed content hanging out with all the horse people at Bar M, but since Karen Hill went under, she was no longer able to ride. I never fully trusted Ebony and Aries was still too young and green.

And then one day, we were on our way to one of Katie's riding lessons. The car was quiet, as usual, until Shannon piped up from the back seat, "Know what I'm going to name my horse when I get him? Mr. Pibb!"

I was immediately overcome with a sense of guilt. (My primary sensation in my life as a parent.) It had never even occurred to me that Shannon would want a horse of her own. That she might want to expand her horse knowledge and abilities, just as her sister had. It furthered deepened my shame that she clearly never thought she needed to ask for a horse. She just assumed that I'd get around to getting her one eventually.

So I went to David Barnett and told him I needed a horse for Shannon. Something bomb-proof.

David regularly attended auctions searching for bargain basement horses for resale. I've never been to a horse auction, but I understand they are much like car auctions. Some people will doctor up a lame horse and run it through an auction, so when the buyer gets their purchase home, they're stuck with a lame horse. Obviously lame or old horses are generally bought by someone who sells them by the pound.

But there are horses at auctions that just legitimately need to find new homes quickly. Horses aren't like selling a car. You can't just stick it in your front yard with a sign on it and forget about it. They still have to eat and they still require your time and care. Some people, when they make the decision to sell a horse, will take them to an auction just to cut the financial drain that would occur if they took the time to try to sell the horse themselves. Those people typically aren't that concerned with whether the horse goes to a good home, or if it ends up on the killer's trailer.

Luckily for us (and him), Shannon's pony-to-be was scooped up by David Barnett with Shannon specifically in mind. He was a sorrel and white pinto gelding, nearly 14 hands high. A hand is equivalent to four inches and is measured from the ground to the top of the withers. Anything under 14 ½ hands is generally considered a pony.

Katie rode him first and pronounced him perfect for Shannon. She was right. Mr. Pibb and Shannon were a match made in heaven. He was easy-going, with no vices at all, but he had enough common sense to keep himself and Shannon out of trouble. He was a babysitter, and a push-button Western pleasure horse.

Shannon had only ridden English at Karen Hill, but the switch to Western suited her. She would groom and tack Pibb herself, and they would ride in the large arena at Bar M. Every. Single. Day.

That year, one of the first Special Olympic Equestrian events in Georgia was held on the campus of Georgia Southern University in Statesboro, Georgia. I was told that Shannon was the youngest participant at 8 years old. Because Karen Hill was no longer really operational, we took Pibb, and also picked up Katie the horse, who had found a new home, but still technically belonged to Karen Hill.

The event was held in an area just a few yards from a major highway, and was fenced off by bright orange plastic construction fencing. The arena consisted of strands of rope with flapping plastic flags ... the kind you see hanging over used-car lots. Horses are not known for their tolerance of unknown moving objects. In the fight or flight response, horses always went for flight, and they went for it quickly. Their speed and quick reaction time was how they survived through centuries of being prey for mountain lions and other swift creatures with claws and teeth.

Therefore, some of the horses trailered in for the event objected to the noise level and spooky moving things. It was not ideal for disabled participants, but it was a learning experience.

I learned that Mr. Pibb was truly unflappable. He didn't even give those flags a second glance. Shannon was as safe on his back as she was in my arms. And Shannon wasn't our only athlete who rode Pibb. He calmly took care of several other members of our Special Olympics team. I don't remember how the scoring went, or what kind of ribbon Shannon brought home, but I do remember that it was a long, exhausting, exhilarating experience.

By this time, we had joined a local organization that held horse shows in nearby Brooks, Georgia. Brooks Saddle Club was part of a larger organization called the Flint River Horseman's Association. The horse shows were open to any breed – any person who wanted to compete. Timed events were the most popular and included barrel racing, pole weaving, basket weaving, and Texas barrels.

There were also Huntseat classes, so Katie would take Ebony and Aries and compete in those. Shannon would go along and watch, and quickly made a few friends. I was certain she would also like to compete, so I talked to Gay Martin, who was the owner of Bar M and who was well-known and influential with the saddle club. I asked her how she thought the members would take it if Shannon competed. There weren't any rules against it, of course, but as usual, I was worried about how people would treat Shannon. I didn't want to expose her to ridicule or embarrassment. Her riding skills were progressing, and Pibb was amazing, but I still didn't think she was on the same level as other kids her age.

Gay spoke to the people at the saddle club and assured me that Shannon would have no problems if she wanted to enter some pony pleasure classes.

The first couple of horse shows we took Shannon to, her name was called last, because she didn't place at all, but they gave her a ribbon anyway. She seemed very happy and I wondered if she realized the difference in ribbons or even understood that she was competing against the other riders. I didn't care. I just wanted to see her happy.

I believe it was only the third show we took her to that something outstanding happened. I was sick that day and watching with only about half my usual enthusiasm. They called the first name and then I heard "Shannon Waldrop." I was confused for a moment, and thought they must be calling the names in reverse order. Then I saw the judge walk up to Shannon and hand her a red ribbon. She had taken second place. The riders waited until all the ribbons had been awarded and then were told to exit the arena.

It was then I knew that Shannon *did* know the difference and she *did* understand that it was a competition. She was the last to leave the arena, and I could see that she had the biggest smile I think I'd ever seen on her face. She turned to leave the arena, and she dropped her reins and gave Pibb a kick, goading him into an instant easy canter. She raised her arms into the air on either side of her and whooped all the way out of the arena.

Even placid Pibb seemed excited, holding his head up a little higher than usual, and people all around the arena were laughing and clapping for them.

Shannon and Pibb quickly became favorites at the horse shows. Everybody knew them. Everybody rooted for them to win. When Shannon and Pibb walked into a class, I noticed that people stopped what they were doing ... stopped practicing their barrel patterns, stopped grilling their hot dogs, stopped grooming their horses ... and watched. When I was out in public with Shannon, people would approach us and start talking to Shannon. People I didn't recognize. This would make me a little nervous, until they would ask Shannon how Mr. Pibb was doing. Then I would relax, realizing that it was someone from the saddle club. It was like having a celebrity in the family.

Shannon and Katie were both racking up blue ribbons right and left. We were at the barn in the fresh air every day, and had horse shows almost every weekend. Shan's motor skills were improving by leaps and bounds, and she was comfortable socializing with anyone, from any background.

And Shannon and Pibb were responsible for my first paid writing job. Their second year of competing with Flint River, they won the year-end award for pony pleasure and pony halter. I was so proud of their accomplishment, I wrote an article about it, stuck it in an envelope and sent it to *Horse Illustrated*. They published it, and paid me for it as well. While I had always been driven to write, and I'd had things published while I was still in school, I'd never been paid for anything I'd written. I was so excited, and Shannon became even more of a celebrity when all her friends from the saddle club read the article.

Joey had also become a fixture at the barn and horse shows. He had no choice but to be a barn baby. At first, he went to the barn in his stroller and would get parked and wheeled around, content with any surroundings as long as his belly was full. Before long, however, he was walking and running, and I was constantly chasing after him. People were always commenting that they didn't understand why I wasn't thin as a rail. Which meant they wondered how I stayed so *fat*, when I was on the move all the time.

While Joey obviously loved being out at the barn, he wasn't as smitten with horses as his sisters. They would occasionally lead him around on Ebony or Pibb, and we even entered him in a couple of lead line classes on Pibb. We would dress him up as an Indian, and put paint on Pibb's face and hindquarters. But I think Joey loved the dressing up part more than the actual riding. He had a vivid imagination, and enjoyed introducing himself as "Cowboy Joey" or "Astronaut Joey" or "Teenage Mutant Ninja Turtle Joey." One day, he ran around the corner of the barn with a towel tucked into the back of his shirt, stopped and planted his fists on his hips and announced loudly, "I am SUPER BM!" Needless to say, everyone within earshot cracked up. I didn't know where he had gotten the "BM" part, until my brother pointed out that it probably stood for "Bar M." In Joey's mind, he was the superhero of the barn, and not the massive bowel movement that everyone else took his clever acronym for.

7 Backbone

"Hey Mom, come here, I need some help."

Katie was in the round pen at Bar M with one of the other boarder's horses. She had grown into quite the barn rat. She spent every minute she could at the barn, and was pretty much David Barnett's right hand man. Whenever someone would come to look at a horse, she would hop into the back of David's pick-up truck, and ride out into the pasture with him and the prospective buyers. He would toss her up bareback and the buyers would be so impressed that an 11-year-old girl could ride the horse bareback that they would be convinced it was the perfect horse for them.

She also picked up extra money around the barn by giving riding lessons and sometimes riding horses for the other boarders. So it wasn't unusual to see her in the round pen with someone else's horse.

I entered the round pen and shut the gate behind me. I walked toward Katie, thinking she needed a leg up. She was generally perfectly capable of mounting on her own, but this horse was a draft-horse cross, tall and muscular.

I cupped my hands and held them out.

"No," Katie said. "Today, *you're* going to ride."

I was immediately seized with a combination of excitement and dread. I couldn't ride. I was too fat.

But Katie knew that I longed to ride. Actually, I longed to ride Aries. My attachment to him had become evident to Katie, and when people would comment on his unparalleled beauty and impeccable manners, she would say, "He's really my mom's horse. She just lets me ride him." My heart would swell a little whenever she said that, but it hurt that I couldn't ride him myself.

"Katie, you know I can't ride. I'm too heavy."

"Nonsense! There are plenty of people heavier than you who ride. Look at Neal."

"Neal's a man. And he's not fat. He's just tall. And muscular."

"So? I bet he weighs more than you. And his horse is a lot smaller than this one."

It was true that Neal's legs looked as if they were going to drag the ground whenever he rode his little mare. But it didn't seem to faze her.

"Well..." I looked around the barnyard to see if anyone else was watching.

"Nobody else is here," Katie said.

"Ok, I guess I'll try."

I move to the horse's side and discovered that the problem of weighing too much for the horse was a moot point if I couldn't get my massive bulk up into the saddle. The horse was really tall. And English saddles don't have a horn to hang onto or pull yourself up on. I would get my foot in the stirrup, but couldn't get enough upward propulsion with my other leg to get into the saddle. I floundered around on that poor horse's side for several long minutes, huffing and puffing. I'd get part of the way up, hang there and then fall back down to the ground. It's a wonder that horse didn't give me a swift kick in the shins to make me stop.

"This isn't going to work," I looked around the barnyard again, just to make sure someone wasn't hiding around the corner, watching my embarrassing display.

Katie let go of the horse's reins to come give me a leg up. She laced her fingers together and held out her cupped hands. "Just put your knee in my hands," she said. "I do it for people all the time."

I knew Katie wasn't going to be able to hoist me up into the saddle the way she did other people, but she was very persistent. So I tried one more time. She had gotten incredibly strong for her age, thanks to countless bales of hay and wheelbarrows full of manure and I was astounded when she was able to get me farther up than I'd gotten myself. With her help, I had almost half my body over the horse's back. I struggled mightily, because I had a brief glimmer of hope, but was unable to get myself into the saddle. I slid back to the ground, my face burning red from exertion and embarrassment.

"Ok," Katie said. "Let's take him out to the mounting block." My daughter didn't believe in giving up on anything.

But I refused. I'd had enough and the horse had surely had enough. And I had decided on a different course of action. One that would take some time.

I come from a long line of extremely large people, at least on my father's side. He had aunts and uncles who weighed over 500 pounds. But while obesity, especially that level of obesity, has long been associated with laziness, these weren't people lying in bed gorging themselves on bon-bons and watching soaps on TV all day long. My aunt Martha was a nurse and her twin brothers Jess and Joe were both truck drivers. My grandmother, who was small compared to some of her siblings, was still a large woman, but she was also one of the hardest-working people I've known. As a farmer's wife, she cooked for large groups of farmhands almost every day. She also cleaned house, canned vegetables, cleaned fish, dressed out deer, and sewed all of her own clothes. And she worked in a shoe factory. To make extra money, she would rise in the wee hours of the morning and make homemade donuts to sell to her coworkers at the factory. I feel sorry for anyone who never got to try one of Grandma's donuts. They were better than hot Krispy Kreme donuts. I swear they were.

And I wasn't exactly a couch potato myself. I worked long hours at the barn, cleaning stalls and turning out horses and loading feed and hay. And while I had a keen appreciation for food, I was always thinking, "But I don't eat that much, either. Look at so-and-so. She eats way more than I do, and she's downright skinny."

But it was clear that drastic action was required if I was ever going to be able to ride. So I embarked on a strict diet that involved pretty much no eating. It wasn't the healthiest course of action, but I was so determined to ride Aries, that I would go for days at a time without eating a bite. And it still seemed to take forever before the weight started to come off.

* * *

Even though I was too heavy to ride Aries, I was happy to groom him and bathe him and feed him apples and just look at him as much as I wanted. Katie was still riding and showing Ebony, but Aries had become her primary hunter/jumper.

As I pulled into the driveway at Bar M one day, I saw a woman we didn't know walking in front the barn. And this woman was leading Aries.

"Who is that?" I asked Katie.

"I don't know," she replied.

"Does she work here?" I thought perhaps Gay, the owner of Bar M, had hired someone new and she had gotten Aries confused with one of the full-board horses – although at the time, he was the only Arabian at Bar M, and would have been difficult to confuse with any other horse there.

We parked and Katie and I got out, leaving Shannon and Joey in the car for the time being and approached the woman.

"Can we help you?" I asked.

"Yes," she replied. "Can you tell me where the tack room is?"

"Why?"

"Because I want to ride," she snapped, her tone indicating that she thought I was an idiot for asking such a question.

I took a deep breath and pushed down the feeling that her tone had provoked, still thinking she must be confused. Maybe she was a new boarder and had bought a horse that looked just like Aries. Although I knew that was impossible, since Aries was the most beautiful horse in the world.

"That's my horse you have there," I said slowly, enunciating so this obviously confused woman could understand.

"No it's not!" Her tone was becoming even more agitated and annoying.

I gritted my teeth and pushed my feelings down again. "Um, yeah it is. This is Aries."

"Yes I know," she said, removing the possibility that she was confusing Aries with some obviously inferior horse.

But now I was the one who was confused. I stood there pondering a response, when she spoke again.

"This is *Jack's* horse," she said in that same contemptible tone. "And he said I could ride him any time I wanted."

And the confusion cleared. I looked down at Katie and said, "Katie, why don't you go back to the car and check on Shannon and Joey for me?"

Katie looked up at me and started to protest, but then she saw the fire in my eyes and decided it would be best not to argue. She turned and went back to the car.

I do not do confrontation well. Not with large, angry men – not with small, annoying women. The fact that my husband was bringing a strange woman to the barn, when he rarely came with me or the kids was a clue that there was something other than mere friendship involved. Add that to the fact that he didn't tell me about it, and factor in past behavior, and I had a pretty good idea of what was going on. But that wasn't what was causing the fire in my eyes.

I took a step closer to the woman, obliterating the sunlight from her skinny little body with my bulk.

I gritted my teeth so hard I think I may have cracked the enamel on at least four or five of them. I leaned forward and I spoke through those clenched teeth.

"Look, lady, I don't care what you do with my *husband*," I said, watching her eyes widen at the word "husband," "but if you ever come near my horse again, I will break every bone in your body."

I watched her face blanch. She was clearly what some people would call feisty, and other people would call a bitch. I was what some people would call soft-hearted, and other people would call a doormat. She was not accustomed to backing down. I was not accustomed to standing up. She wanted to formulate a comeback. I could read it there in her eyes. But she also saw something in my eyes. And I was twice her size. At least.

I would never have actually broken her bones. I would usher spiders out of my house with a piece of paper when I could, rather than squash them. But she didn't know that.

I held out my hand, and with nothing but a small sputter of indignation, she turned over Aries' lead rope. And she got in her car with the trash bag taped over the window and she drove away, never to be seen again.

As I watched the car disappear down the driveway, I was surprised to realize that I was completely calm. My hands weren't shaky and I didn't have that sick feeling in the pit of my stomach that generally accompanied any interaction that could remotely be construed as confrontational. I didn't even like playing chess because you had to "attack" your opponent.

And yet, I felt perfectly fine after threatening another person with bodily harm. I looked at Aries, who was regarding me with what I imagined to be great admiration and gratitude for saving him from that horrid woman. I patted his neck and motioned for Katie to get out of the car. The second David arrived at the barn, we were going to ask to move Aries to a new stall.

8 NAVICULAR

SOMETHING was wrong with Mr. Pibb. Probably the people who took him to that auction knew it, and were trying to get rid of him before it became more obvious.

You should always have a horse vetted before you buy it. Always. And yet, I'm so glad we didn't. Because if we'd done the sensible thing, the fiscally smart thing, we probably would have found out that Mr. Pibb had navicular disease. We might have passed on him, and Shannon would have missed out on a great experience. And a great friend.

Navicular disease is a degenerative disorder of the hoof, and can cause lameness in the front feet. It is probably best compared to carpal tunnel syndrome in people. But people don't have to walk on their hands.

Pibb seemed completely sound for the first couple of years that we had him. But then he started having problems. He would seem fine walking around, but if Shannon asked him to trot or canter, he would refuse. We had our vet check him out and got the diagnosis. There was and still is a lot of debate about causes and treatments, but for Pibb, lots of pasture rest was definitely in order. Shan could still ride him around at a walk occasionally, but his days of competition were over.

Having a good farrier is paramount to keeping a horse with navicular sound for as long as possible. Horse's feet grow constantly, just like our fingernails, and they have to be trimmed periodically, to keep them from getting too long. That's where farriers come in.

How often you see the farrier varies depending on how much the horse is turned out, what kind of work they do, and what kind of terrain exists in their pasture. That's because a hoof will wear down somewhat naturally as a horse moves and grazes in a pasture. The harder and rockier the pasture setting, the faster the hoof wears down. Horses that are stalled won't wear down their hooves in that manner and will probably require more frequent trims. Also, just because a horse's hoof wears down, doesn't mean it wears down evenly. Just like people, some horses walk with more weight on the inside, outside, front or back of their feet. This uneven wear can also lead to problems with muscles and tendons. So those horses may also require more frequent trims. And some horses do better with shoes, also depending on their workload, environment, and anatomy.

Horses with navicular often have low heels and long toes, which was true in Pibb's case. He had shoes on when we bought him, but we had them pulled off, which very likely could have accounted for the extra couple of years of use we got out of him. Some people believe that letting a horse with navicular go barefoot promotes blood flow and improves healing.

I wanted to do whatever I could to make Pibb comfortable. He had given Shannon so many happy hours and he deserved the best care possible.

We had a regular farrier, but as Pibb's feet got worse, I decided to try a new farrier that someone had recommended as being really good at trimming and shoeing horses with navicular. He was a large, ruddy fellow who worked somewhat slowly and talked a lot. It probably took him twenty minutes to finish Pibb's front feet before he started on his hind feet.

"He's being particular," I thought. "Doing a good job, so Pibb's feet won't hurt him as much." I thought the extra time he was spending (and the extra money I was paying) would pay off in extra comfort for Pibb.

The problem was that all that time the new farrier was working, Pibb was having to stand on three legs. And two of his legs were already hurting.

So when the farrier started on his hind leg, Pibb started leaning against him. He was just trying to get a little weight off his painful front feet, but it was uncomfortable for the farrier to have a seven-hundred-pound pony leaning against him.

The farrier pushed Pibb back a couple of times, setting his hind foot down and straightening up. I knew it must hurt his back to stay bent over for so long, trimming Pibb's feet. But he was becoming obviously agitated.

After a few minutes, the guy just lost it. He dropped Pibb's foot and cursed loudly, and turning around, swung the large metal rasp he was using as hard as he could into Pibb's rib cage. The sound it made echoed throughout the barn, and Pibb tried to jump away from him, to the side, hobbling a bit on his sore feet.

As I've said, I do not handle confrontation well. And I especially do not handle confrontation with large, angry men well. But as Popeye would say, "That's all I can stands, I can't stands no more."

As calmly as possible, I walked up and snapped Pibb's lead line onto his halter.

The farrier glowered at me angrily. "What? I didn't hurt him none. Just taught him ta not lean on me, that's all!"

I ignored him and released Pibb's halter from the cross ties.

"I only done three legs!" the guy protested.

"It's ok," I said. "I'll pay you for four." I handed him the check I had already made out, and I led Pibb, with his lopsided trim job, out to the pasture gate.

I called our regular farrier the second I got home, and apologized profusely for even considering using anyone else.

* * *

Pibb was out of commission, but Shannon still wanted to ride in Special Olympics. By now, she had done three State Special Olympic Games on Pibb and her riding skills had progressed by leaps and bounds. Aries had also matured and progressed, having been through untold number of horse shows with Katie.

So we decided that it would be all right for Shannon to ride Aries in Special Olympics. That year, the event was held in Warm Springs, Georgia, where Franklin Roosevelt's "Little White House" is located.

Event organizers had learned a lot in the years since that first Special Olympics, and this one was held on the grounds of a therapeutic riding program, much like Karen Hill. There was a permanent arena made of wooden rails, not flapping flags, the number of participants had grown, and several members of the media were on hand to document the event.

Most of the horses used were program horses like the ones from Karen Hill. Aries was probably about nine years old by this time, but he was a youngster compared to most of the horses there. He definitely stood out.

Shannon's first class was trail riding. It was held in the indoor arena, and consisted of an obstacle course that horse and rider had to navigate. They had to walk over wooden rails on the ground, maneuver through a path of cones, back up, go through a gate, and Shannon even had to open a mailbox from Aries' back. Aries didn't miss a step, and they took a gold medal in that class.

The second class they were in was a walk/trot class that was to be held later in the afternoon. We relaxed at the trailer and talked about perhaps visiting nearby Callaway Gardens when the competition was over.

Mother Nature had other plans, however, as it soon started to drizzle, and then turned into a downpour. The walk/trot class was supposed to have been held in the outdoor arena, but the rain forced everyone inside.

The barn was extremely crowded and noisy, and it had a tin roof, which makes a terrible racket in a rainstorm. Aries was never fond of rainstorms. I always thought it was because of Margaret's story of his birth. I can imagine that it would be quite a shock, being in a warm dark womb, and then suddenly thrust into a world of cold, pelting raindrops, flashing lightning and booming thunder.

Competitors all had side walkers, who were allowed to have a lead line attached to the bridle. Most, if not all, of the other riders did this. However, Shannon and Aries had done so well in the trail class earlier, without a lead line, that I thought they would surely be ok in this class. After all, it was a much easier class.

But I wasn't accounting for the rain. I should have noticed that Aries was tense, but I didn't. So the class began, and I was walking beside Aries, sans lead line, when I put a hand on his shoulder and felt him jump just a little. I finally looked at him ... really looked ... and realized how stressed he was. I listened to all the noise in the barn, all the people crowding in out of the rain, standing along the rail. I could even hear some piglets squealing in the background. No wonder he was tense! He was doing his best to be calm and controlled, but I could see a disaster looming. Shannon had a pretty good seat and could handle a small buck or spook, but a full-out bolt would most likely unseat her. As we walked along the rail, I spotted Katie and bent underneath Aries' neck and hissed at her, "Lead line. Now, please!"

I don't know how she got through that crowd and back with a lead line so fast, but we hadn't gone halfway around the arena before Katie materialized, tossing a bunched-up lead line to me over the railing. I snapped it to Aries' bit and relaxed just a little.

Then we rounded a corner, and I saw that a television reporter had decided to climb onto the railing of the arena to get better shots. He was leaning over the railing, his back toward us, shooting the riders in front of us as they walked away. Aries wasn't just the youngest horse in the competition, he was also probably the tallest, and as we approached the cameraman, the guy decided to swing his camera around to film us coming toward him. That's when I saw that he had an enormous, incredibly bright light attached to the top of his camera. And it was shining directly into Aries' eyes.

What happened next felt much worse than it looked, I'm sure. Aries' head went up in the air, his hooves doing a staccato pattern in the dirt, his hindquarters squatting down, preparing to propel him as far away from that bright light and all those crazy sounds as he could get. I moved my grip on the lead line closer to his bridle and put my hand against his shoulder, moving as close as I dared. I had to shout his name for him to hear me over the noise. "Aries! Whoa, boy! Whoa! It's ok!"

I saw the white around Aries' eye as he looked at me. I could feel him trembling under my hand. In my peripheral vision, I could see the cameraman lean back and climb down from his perch, hopefully having realized his mistake. I wanted to look at Shannon, to make sure she was ok, but I couldn't take my eyes off Aries. I had to get through to him. His next few steps were quick, his legs drilling hard into the ground, as if he thought he could punch a hole through the arena floor and escape, his head still high in the air. But slowly, he calmed down, and I was able to shoot a quick glance upward at Shannon.

Her eyes were straight ahead, not looking at me at all. She was focused on the task at hand and she was trusting Aries and me to work out this little episode and finish the class. If she had been worried in the least, it didn't show on her face.

By the time the riders lined up in the center of the arena to await the judge's decision, my legs were shaking, and it wasn't from the little bit of jogging I'd had to do when the judge asked for a trot. I was drained, and I could still feel the tension emanating from Aries. I asked Shannon to go ahead and dismount, because I thought that Aries had had about as much as he could take for one day. They got a bronze medal in that class, and I was so proud of Aries for holding it together and of Shannon for being so darned unflappable.

9 KHAN

IT was around this time that we left Bar M after five years of boarding there. David Barnett had taken a job at another stable and wanted us to come with him. He offered to let Katie work off our boarding bill if she moved with him.

I wasn't so sure. Like Shannon, I didn't always handle change well. I guess because I'd had so much upheaval and uncertainty in my life, I tended to cling to the known. I was a bit worried about jumping from the frying pan into the fire … although that's not the best analogy, since I was content at Bar M. I don't think there is an adage for going from a good situation to one that's just not quite so good, though. Maybe I should make one up. Like, "going from a Lazy Boy to a straight-backed chair." I was comfortable at Bar M, and wasn't sure a new barn would be a good fit.

However, I changed my mind the moment I laid eyes on Rock House Ranch. I think that perhaps there are places on this earth, small pockets of harmony composed of dirt and grass and trees that speak to me and ease my worry and pain. Maybe it's my farming family roots. I don't know.

I do know that when I first pulled into that driveway, and saw the old red barn on my left, and a sweeping pasture with a majestic stand of good Georgia pecan trees on the right, I felt enveloped by peace. This was my place. I just knew it. There was happiness waiting for me here.

The original part of the barn, I was told, used to be a peach packing facility. Then someone added old boxcars to the outside of the building, forming stalls. An iron silhouette of a train was attached to the side of the barn, as an homage to this bit of history.

We brought five horses to Rock House. In addition to Aries, Mr. Pibb, and Ebony, we had acquired a paint filly whose registered name was "Dude's Jolly Boots," but we just called her Filly. Katie chose "Philadelphia Freedom" as Filly's show name, so she could tell people that "Filly" was short for "Philadelphia."

The other addition to our herd was a straight Egyptian Arabian stallion we had gotten from Al Koger. His registered name was Ramses Ali Khan, and his sire, Ruminaja Ali, was U.S. National Champion Futurity Colt in 1979. There are different strains of purebred Arabians, based upon the part of the world in which they were bred, and while they all share Arabian traits, each strain has its own unique characteristics. Aries came from Polish lines. His great-grandsire was a famous Polish Arabian named Bask. Bask was a U.S. National Champion Stallion and Park Horse. Polish Arabians tend to be bigger and heavier than Egyptian Arabians. Aries was probably a full hand taller than Khan.

Like most straight Egyptians, Khan was compact and exotic, with a long wavy mane and enormous eyes. His eyes were so prominent, in fact, that he always seemed to be skinning up his eye socket on something. The first time I saw him, he had banged his eye on the edge of the horse trailer as he backed out at Bar M. It was dripping blood down his stunningly gorgeous dished face.

Khan was about three when we got him. He was bred at Talaria Farms, an Arabian farm in Newnan. Talaria was where Katie had her first official job. When Khan came to us, he had been turned out in a pasture for several months with a gelding, a mare, and another stallion. The other stallion was older and much bigger, and Khan had bite marks all over him that told a clear story of competition over the prize of the only mare in the pasture.

Khan wasn't large in stature, but he was enormous with attitude. He was wild and full of life and brimming over with energy. When we put him in a stall, he would constantly walk in circles, or weave back and forth in the front of the stall. When we turned him out in a paddock, he would run or trot up and down the fence line for hours on end. He could work up a sweat in zero degree weather. While Aries had convinced some of the Bar M folks that Arabians could be calm and sane, Khan seemed determined to reinforce the "crazy" Arabian stereotype. People would just watch his antics in the pasture and shake their heads. They saw crazy, but I saw pure, unadulterated joy and beauty.

And maybe to prove them wrong, or maybe because I still didn't know enough about horses to make a sensible decision, or maybe because I just had too much confidence in her abilities, I let my 11-year-old daughter break and train him.

Looking back on it, I feel guilty for being so reckless with her safety. Looking back, I cringe, knowing what could have happened to her. But what actually did happen was magical, in my admittedly biased opinion.

Months later, I stood by the rail at Katie's first A-rated Arabian show. Because we didn't have registration papers for Aries, she had been unable to show him at Arabian shows. That was fine, because she just did hunter /jumper shows instead. However, she wanted to show at the big Arabian shows, and Khan gave her the ability to do that.

Standing beside me on the rail was the mother of one of the other competitors. She pointed out her daughter and asked me which one was mine. I felt her silent judgment when I pointed Katie out to her. It was a Western Pleasure class, and most of the competitors had saddles and bridles dripping with silver. Those saddles and bridles cost several thousands of dollars. The chaps and outfits could cost hundreds more. Katie was riding in a plain saddle and bridle, with only a few small silver embellishments. She had even had to borrow a hat for the show, one that was just a tad too big for her. In terms of money, we were extremely outclassed, a fact that other mother let me know right away. She told me how much she paid for her daughter's mare, which was more than I could earn in 10 years of working. Then she told me how much she paid their trainer, how much she paid for the saddle, how much she paid for her daughter's custom-made chaps, her hat, her shirt and her gloves. I stood in silence, my heart aching because I couldn't give my daughter all that, and I had foolishly allowed her to train her own horse (A stallion! My stars!) and had scraped up the entry fees to this show in which she was going to be embarrassed and humiliated.

And then the riders entered the arena. And at the very moment Katie and Khan were entering, a loose dog ran right underneath Khan's legs. My heart sank even further, even more convinced this was a mistake. Who did we think we were? We didn't belong here, with these people.

Khan skittered sideways, tilting his head downward to give the dog an evil look. But then Katie took control, and Khan's lovely movement kicked in. They were breathtaking. Literally. I could not breathe. I had never witnessed a horse and rider so in sync, so perfect. It was downright artistic. I stood riveted, tuning out the other mother's chatter. I didn't care if Katie came in last at that moment. I knew what an incredible job she had done, training a horse no one thought she should, entering a show that was out of our league. Screw them all, I thought. I don't care if she wins. This is beautiful.

At the end of the class, the competitors all lined up, waiting for the results, the lights of the arena glinting off all that silver. I could see how a judge might be blinded by all that bling, and I resigned myself to giving Katie a speech about how awesome she was and how the opinion of the judge didn't matter so much as her determination and how far she had come with Khan.

But that was one speech I didn't have to give. Because my daughter, in her plain saddle and borrowed hat, on a giveaway horse that she trained herself, took home a blue ribbon that day.

I didn't say a word to that other mother, but I admit I did look her directly in the eye for the first time that day. I probably hitched my chin up a bit. Maybe my smile was a tad smug. Surprisingly, she also seemed to be at a loss for words. Finally. She stormed away, and I was sure her trainer was about to get an earful.

* * *

The horses all seemed to enjoy Rock House as much as I did. It quickly became my haven and my inspiration. I was still trying to lose weight, and the pasture at Rock House was the perfect place to walk. It was approximately a mile down the fence line to the lake at the back of the property, and I walked it every single day, rain or shine, cold or blistering heat.

I had a tiny cassette player that I would hang on my belt and put my headphones on. At the time, I was listening mostly to Garth Brooks and our own homegrown hero, Alan Jackson, who was from nearby Newnan, Georgia. The music helped motivate me to keep going and I began to see the pounds melt off. Step by step, I was getting closer to my dream of riding Aries. As I walked, I could see it in my mind, going on long trail rides and collecting blue ribbons of my own. It was so close I could taste it.

10 HOOCH

DAVID Barnett had a saying, "Buy a horse, get a divorce."
There did seem to be some credence to his theory. Seldom were both partners equally enamored of their new equine family members. One partner (most often the female partner) would begin spending more and more time at the barn and less time with their significant other. This could lead to friction, jealousy, arguments over money, etc. But then again, with the divorce rate upwards of 50%, it's more likely that horses were just an excuse for some people.

Horses did not cause my divorce. At least not directly. But I did find myself alone after 16 years of marriage. Suddenly, I was on my own, with no job, no income, no money, and nowhere to live.

So I moved into my brother's basement. This was not a finished basement, mind you. The floors were concrete and there were pipes and electrical wires running through the roof above us. The first night, the three kids and me all crowded into our one bed, and Joey looked up at those pipes and wires and exclaimed, "Living in the basement is going to be cool!" Oh, to look at life through those optimistic eyes.

Because living in the basement was most decidedly not cool. My brother and his girlfriend were not pleased to have us and our dogs squatting in their basement. And who could blame them? We were noisy and messy and the dogs were smelly. And we hated being there even more than they hated having us there.

Desperate to get out of there and support my kids, I got a job waiting tables at a little place called C&D's Pizzeria during the day. For a person with social anxiety, waiting tables has to be one of the most tortuous professions possible. You are forced to greet a new person every few minutes. And sometimes those people aren't nice. But I had to take care of my kids and my critters, so I had to do it.

However, my job at C&D's didn't bring in nearly enough money, so I got another job waiting tables at night, at Shoney's. I would get up at 6 a.m., get the kids off to school, go to my first job, work through lunch, pick the kids up, take them home and try to feed them something, and then go to Shoney's. I typically got out of there around 1 a.m., and would drive the half hour home and crash on the floor beside the kid's bed. The four of us sleeping in one bed just didn't work. None of us got any sleep. But because those floors were concrete, I had soon worn big sores on both my hips. It was one down side to losing weight. Before, my hips were nice and padded, but their new boniness made for some real discomfort when forced to lie against concrete every night.

We had moved to the basement in September, and the next few months were a stressful blur. Christmas Eve, I got a call at work. Aries was colicking. Thankfully, Shoney's closed early on Christmas Eve and was closed on Christmas Day. For three years running, my only day off of the entire year was Christmas Day. I worked one job or the other or both every single day, 364 days. That year was just the beginning.

I got out of work as early as I could and drove as fast as my rattletrap car would go straight to Rock House. Our vet, Johnny Pritchard, was already there and had Aries on the wash rack. He had been oiled and walked and given Banamine for pain. All we could do was watch him and wait for him to poop.

Horses have rather delicate digestive systems. They eat pretty much non-stop, like most grazing animals. So food moves through in constant, but small quantities. Too much food at one time, or strange food or stress … any of those can cause a horse to colic. Often, in order to get relief from the pain in their gut, horses will roll violently. This thrashing about can cause injury or a dreaded torsion … the twisting of a part of their intestines that will not allow waste to pass through as usual. This can lead to an extremely painful death. The appearance of poop is a good sign that there is no torsion or blockage, so a horse owner with a colicky horse celebrates those stinky balls as if they were pure gold nuggets dropping to the ground.

Johnny stayed with me on the wash rack until well after dark, then left me with a vial of Banamine and a promise that he would be back in the morning. Aries wasn't out of the woods, but seemed relatively comfortable, so I put him in his stall beside the wash rack and then stood in the corner, just watching him and praying for poop.

After about an hour, the door to the stall slid open and Katie was standing there with an odd expression on her face. I was preoccupied with Aries, of course, and didn't even notice that she appeared to have some sort of bundle in her arms.

"Mom?" she was almost whispering. "I have something for you." She held her arms out, and that was when I saw a black nose and two shiny black eyes peering out of a ball of fluffy fur. "Merry Christmas," she said. I was numb with stress and worry, and my first thought was "My brother will kill me if I bring another dog home. He's already unhappy with the dogs we have now."

Years earlier, I had seen a video on *Sesame Street*. A song called "Hard-workin' Dog" played while a black and white dog rounded up cattle and leapt into a pickup truck with astounding ease. I had never seen a dog like that, and I wanted one badly. I did some research and found out that it was a border collie, a herding breed that originated in Scotland. Today, border collies are quite familiar and common in the United States, but at that time, they were still a relatively rare breed here. I had never seen one in person or knew anyone who had owned one. This was, of course, before the film *Babe* made them popular.

But one day, my daughter was riding past a house that sat on the edge of the Rock House property. And she saw a woman giving commands to a black and white dog. She was impressed with the dog's obvious intelligence and eagerness to please, and stopped to chat with the woman. When she found out the dog was a border collie, she told the woman about how much her mother wanted a border. Katie asked her to let her know if she ever decided to breed her dog, because she would like to buy a puppy. The woman said she didn't have any plans to breed her dog, because she used her in herding competitions. As fate would have it, however, the dog was spending some time with a border collie trainer and accidentally had a romantic interlude with the trainer's stud dog. Katie got the pick of the litter, and he happened to be about weaning age right at Christmas.

Fate dropped this gift into my lap, but at the time, I was too miserable to appreciate it. It's one of those moments that I would change if I could go back in time. I would hug Katie tightly and tell her how much I appreciated her thoughtfulness and caring. I would tell her that this puppy would grow up to be the best dog we'd ever have. That we would love him and he would love us and protect us with the ferocity of a family member. But I didn't do any of that. I said the first thing that came to my mind, and that was "We can't take another dog back to that basement." I immediately kicked myself for the hurt look that entered my daughter's eyes and I tried to smooth it over. We'd figure it out. I appreciated it. Yes, he was very cute. But the worry grew, and the weight on my shoulders felt as if it would crush me.

Aries continued to show signs of mild colic throughout Christmas Day. Dr. Pritchard came back and hooked an IV up to him on the wash rack. I will never forget JP's kindness and dedication. How many vets will go to such extraordinary lengths … even giving up their Christmas holiday? By that evening, however, Aries was markedly improved, and JP pronounced him out of the woods. He drove off to enjoy leftovers with his family, and Katie and I were finally able to leave Aries and take our new puppy home.

We christened the new pup "Pirate of the Chattahoochee" … Hooch for short. He joined our dogs Twinkie, a retriever mix dog that we had rescued from a dumpster, and Muffin, an aging small ball of fluff that we'd had since the girls were only three or four years old.

11 Homeless

I was trying to be quiet. One thing my brother's girlfriend complained about was that we were too noisy, often disturbing her sleep. So when I arrived home from Shoney's after midnight, I would ease myself into the kitchen and then tiptoe down the stairs.

The dogs greeted me with enthusiasm as usual, and I whispered my return greetings and ruffled their ears, taking care not to get them too worked up and noisy.

After greeting me, Twinkie ran to the basement door and looked back at me expectantly.

"Oh, you need to go out?" I whispered. I moved to the door and opened it, stepping outside to keep an eye on Twinkie. She trotted over to the edge of the yard to relieve herself, while I leaned against the side of the house, my back and legs aching from a long day at work.

I heard a noise near the front of the house and stepped around the corner. I was surprised to see my brother's mastiff, YD (short for "Yard Dog"). It was unusual to see her here, in the unfenced front portion of the yard. She and the Rottweiler that belonged to my brother's girlfriend were usually in the fenced portion of the backyard.

YD was just as surprised to see me, but she was overjoyed. YD was an extremely shy dog, but I was familiar to her and she was fond of me. And so that hundred-pound bundle of fur and slobber was suddenly hurtling my way joyously.

Twinkie, however, wasn't familiar with YD, as my dogs were confined to the basement. She also wasn't sure of this strange dog's intentions, and bravely flung her beautiful golden body between me and impending attack. YD was taken by surprise and initially knocked off her feet, Twinkie standing over her glowering.

That tide turned quickly, however, as YD's forty-pound advantage went to work. She was angry and frightened by this unwarranted attack and was serious about inflicting as much damage as possible. She was also deaf to my voice. The growling and teeth and thrashing about was terrifying. YD soon had Twinkie on the ground, her teeth clenched tightly on Twinkie's neck.

Fearful for Twinkie's life, I straddled YD's body and put both my arms around her front legs in a sort of hammer hold and pulled up as hard as I could. I managed to pull her up, but her jaws were locked onto Twinkie's neck so tightly that I just pulled both of them with me. Terrified, I let go and went scrambling up the stairs, screaming for my brother. He didn't feel the urgency to save Twinkie's life that I did, but he did come and one command from him sent YD off.

He stomped back upstairs, clearly angry at having his sleep disturbed again and I brought Twinkie inside and examined her wounds. I found that her neck wounds were superficial. Her uncertain breeding, being a dumpster dog, had endowed her with a beautiful creamy neck ruff, intimating at a collie in her family tree. That creamy ruff was now stained with blood, but the real injury was a nasty gash on one of her forelegs. No way could I afford another vet bill, so I cleaned it up as best I could and put some ointment on it. And I prayed.

* * *

The following night, I came home, tiptoeing in as usual, making my way to the basement door. But I never made it.

My brother was waiting up for me. And he'd been drinking. His girlfriend had left him. Left him because of his kindness in letting me, my kids, and my dogs live in their basement for six months for only $100 a month and half the utilities. I guess the incident with the dogs the night before was the last straw. My brother was hurt and angry and his anger was directed, of course, at me. He wanted me out. Right then.

As miserable as we were in that basement, I was terrified of living on my own, and I had no money to go anywhere else.

So I tried to reason with him. Then I foolishly tried to argue with him. Stand up to him. I knew better. I knew that would only fuel his anger. But I was tired. I hadn't slept at all the night before and I wasn't thinking clearly.

When I saw him draw his fist back, I braced myself. No one had struck me in many years. My marriage wasn't perfect by any stretch of the imagination, but there was no way my ex-husband would have ever hit me. Or allowed anyone else to do so. But before he came along, I had been a punching bag, and I'd learned how to take it. How to send my mind away and not feel the pain until later. So my reaction when I saw the cocked fist was to brace and prepare.

But then, out of nowhere, my daughter stepped in. Katie flung herself between my brother and me the same way Twinkie had flung herself between YD and me. Life had changed. I had protectors. And I had to protect them.

* * *

I love my brother. In fact, I adore him. I admire him. And I always will. We've been through things together that no one else on the planet can understand. And although we had those same experiences, my brother and I developed distinctly different coping mechanisms. It can all be boiled down to the decision between flight or fight. I was a zebra. I most often chose flight. He was a lion. He most often chose fight. Those differences meant that we could only co-exist as long as nothing pushed either of us into going for our coping mechanisms. Which in turn meant that there have been long periods of my life in which I did not see or talk to my brother. Other times, I don't know what I'd have done without him.

* * *

"No!" I pushed Katie back. "No." I said more calmly. "We'll leave." I was a zebra. I knew how to run. I didn't know where we'd go, but I knew I couldn't allow any harm to come to my children.

I started toward the carport door, but he blocked my way. "You can't take the car," he said. He had given me the car, so he felt justified in denying it to me.

I put my arm around Katie and pushed her toward the basement door. We'd get a few things and go out that way. As we walked down the steep stairs, he shouted down, "And if you don't take your dogs, I'll kill them!"

And so I found myself homeless, kicked out in the middle of the night with nowhere to go.

Luckily, Shannon and Joey were spending the weekend with their father, so I only had to worry about Katie and the dogs.

Twinkie, however, was unable to walk, because of the leg injury she'd gotten the night before in her encounter with YD. But I couldn't leave her there. Loyalty goes both ways. So I hoisted her into my arms, and Katie leashed the other two and we walked out into the night.

The house was in a relatively rural area, so I didn't have to worry about any neighbors seeing or hearing us. There wasn't a lot of traffic, either. Or street lights.

Katie and I made our way to the road and crossed over to the other side, where there weren't as many houses. Instead, there was a large wooded area to our right.

We probably didn't even get a mile when we heard a car coming from behind us ... from the direction of the house we'd just fled. And I panicked.

My moment of bravado from earlier had vanished, replaced by my customary cowardice and fear. Was it my brother, coming after us? Was he still angry? And even if it wasn't my brother, who else would be driving down our road that late at night, and how would they react to seeing a woman and a teenage girl walking by themselves?

Terrified, I hustled us off the side of the road, sliding down an embankment, and lying down flat until the headlights passed.

Lying on my back in the grass, with Twinkie on my chest, I looked at my daughter hunkered down, cradling the dogs she loved, and I felt like the worst mother in the world. Who puts their kid in this kind of position? Who puts their *dogs* in this kind of position? What a loser.

Katie, of course, was the picture of calm composure.

"Mom," she said after the car had passed. "You're not going to make it much farther carrying Twinkie. Let's just go over in the woods and wait for daylight."

She was right. My legs were shaking from exhaustion and exertion. And so we moved off into the woods, far enough so that no one could see us from the road. Katie curled up on the ground with Hooch and Muffin beside her, and I sat with my back against a tree, Twinkie's head resting in my lap.

I sat there the rest of the night, straining my eyes into the dark to watch for dangers. Bears or snakes or people.

As soon as it was daylight, I left Katie in the woods with the dogs and I walked to a convenience store to use the payphone. As I stood with my hand on that hunk of black plastic, the tagline from a recent movie ran through my head. "Who you gonna call?"

As stressed and exhausted as I was, I giggled at the thought. My first call was to Rock House Ranch. Katie occasionally babysat for Chris and Mona's little boy, and they had a spare bedroom that she usually stayed in. I can't remember what story I gave them, but I know it wasn't the truth. At least not the whole truth. I was too embarrassed. I think I just asked if Katie and the dogs could stay with them for a while. They agreed without hesitation.

My second call was to my ex-husband. As humiliating as it was, I told him the whole story. He agreed to let Shannon and Joey stay with him, and he said he'd come pick Katie and the dogs up and take them to Rock House for me.

Now I just had to figure out what to do about me. I made a couple of calls, but the unhesitating offer of help that I received for my kids was harder to find for me. There were people who cared about my kids. Me, not so much.

I hung up the phone and headed back to Katie. It was a three or four mile hike back to where she was hidden in the woods with the dogs. I needed to hustle if I was going to get to her before her father showed up. I'd given him a general vicinity, but I'd also told her not to come out of the woods, so I needed to get there or he wouldn't be able to find her.

They were waiting patiently exactly where I'd left them, and together we walked nearer to the edge of the woods, to watch for the truck.

When I saw it, I stepped out from among the trees and waved, and Jack did a u-turn in the middle of the road, pulled to the side and got out.

"Are you ok?" he asked. "Do I need to kick anybody's ass?"

I shook my head, fighting off the urge to grab him and beg him to take care of me again. He was already remarried, which had happened pretty much immediately upon our divorce. I was going to have to figure a way out on my own.

I struggled to lift Twinkie into his pickup, and he reached out to help me. Twinkie snarled and snapped at him. He jerked his hand back.

"I guess she doesn't remember me," he said.

"It's just been a long night for all of us," I apologized, sending mental messages to Twinkie to please calm down and go with him. She was just being protective, but he'd never been fond of the dogs. If he changed his mind about taking them, I didn't know what I'd do.

But he was too worried about Katie to care much about the dogs, and soon they were all loaded up and ready to go. Jack knew Chris and Mona, and knew that Katie would be safe at their house, but maybe he was also a little worried about me.

"What are you going to do?" he asked awkwardly.

"I'll be fine. I'm sure he's calmed down now. I'll go back to the house. I just don't want the kids there. You understand, right?" I knew he wouldn't have let the kids go back there anyway. I suspect he knew I wasn't going to stay there, either, but what else could he do? I wasn't his responsibility anymore.

And so I stood and watched the truck drive off with a big portion of everything I held dear. And I started walking back toward the house.

I didn't see my brother's truck in the driveway, so I breathed a little easier. Still, I went in through the basement door and was as quiet as possible. He could still be there. I took a couple of big garbage bags and shoved a bunch of clothes into them. I threw them over my shoulder like I was Santa Claus and I headed up the stairs.

I still had my keys in my pocket, and was thankful that my brother hadn't demanded that I turn them over the night before. At the top of the stairs, I held my breath for a moment, gathering my courage in case I opened the door to an angry person blocking my path.

The house was quiet, and as far as I could tell, no one was home. Still, I hurried to the carport door and threw my garbage bags of clothes into my back seat and with shaking hands, turned the ignition, praying that the car would start. It did.

Now I just had to get to work. I drove to a truck stop and went inside and asked for the key to the restroom. I rummaged through my garbage bags until I found some work clothes for C&Ds. My uniform there consisted simply of a pair of jeans and a Braves t-shirt. Best uniform ever. Simple. Functional. Cheap.

I dressed in the bathroom and I went to work. And after work, I drove to the same truck stop and changed into my Shoney's uniform.

I had become somewhat friendly with one of the other servers at Shoney's. Wendy had horses, she was divorced, we were about the same age, and we seemed to have a lot in common. I had been to her apartment a couple of times, and I knew her kids lived with her ex-husband. So I thought that maybe if I shared my situation with her, she would offer to let me crash on her couch for a little while.

Although she was extremely sympathetic, she didn't offer to let me stay with her. I moved through the night in a fog, taking orders, cleaning tables … going through the motions, for once actually dreading the end of my shift, not knowing where I would go afterward.

And then Wendy came to me smiling. She said she had come up with a solution to my problem. His name was Martin.

Martin was a regular at Shoney's. He came in almost every night, and tipped generously. He was an older man, but trim and athletic, with gray hair and a pencil-thin moustache.

Wendy said that Martin would let me stay at his house until I figured out what to do. I was mortified. I would never have shared my situation with one of our customers. And yet, I was also grateful. Martin seemed like a really nice man, and it was so kind of him to offer to help me.

Martin hung around until after close so I could follow him to his house. It was only a few minutes away, a small ranch-style house on a rural road, bordered by a ramshackle white picket fence.

I pulled in behind Martin's car and got out. I started to get one of my garbage bags of clothing out, but changed my mind for some reason.

He opened the door and ushered me inside.

"Let me show you around," he said, taking me by the elbow.

There wasn't much to show. The living room was on my right, with a worn leather couch and a television set. The kitchen area was on the left, with formica countertops and a metal 60s era table and chairs.

But he wasn't interested in showing me the kitchen or living room. He opened a door and stepped in, pulling me with him.

"This is the bedroom," he said.

"It's nice," I said, glancing around at the bedroom, which wasn't actually particularly nice, but did look comfortable. I wondered if he was going to sleep on the couch and let me have the bedroom, and that's why he was showing it to me with such a flourish.

I could feel his eyes on me, and so I turned and looked at him in puzzlement. I was missing something.

And then he leaned in to kiss me. And suddenly, belatedly, the light dawned.

At that point in my life, I had only ever been intimate with one person ... my husband. Any person with a modicum of common sense would have known the score. But not me. No sireebob. I just thought, "What a great guy. It's so nice to know there are still good people around. People who will help you, out of the goodness of their hearts."

I drew back, a wave of shock and despair sweeping over me.

"What's the matter?" he asked. He was annoyed.

And I felt his hand tighten on my arm. And I felt a band of fear tighten around my heart.

I stammered, "Oh, I'm so sorry ... I didn't realize ... I didn't think ... I mean I thought ..."

His eyes hardened, and he dropped my arm.

"You thought I'd just let you stay here for nothing?" his voice dripped with sarcasm.

I stepped back, out of the bedroom, into the relative safety of the living room. I cast a longing look at that weary-looking leather couch.

"Couldn't I just sleep on the sofa?" I asked in a tiny stupid voice. "I wouldn't be any trouble, I promise."

A little bit of the annoyance left his face. I think he may have felt a tiny bit sorry for me. But not sorry enough to let me stay under his roof for free.

"No. You either sleep with me or you leave."

* * *

When I was a teenager, I went on a double date with a friend. A blind date. I thought it was funny that she'd asked me along, as we were more acquaintances than friends. I didn't really have friends. And I thought we were going to the movies, but instead we drove to a tiny backroad in the middle of a bayou and parked.

My friend and her boyfriend immediately got busy in the front seat, and my date began pawing at me. I had only met him twenty minutes before. When I tried to push him away, he got more and more aggressive, attempting to pin my arms down against my side as he thrust his tongue into my mouth. And so I bit him.

Shocked and angry, he slapped me. It was a girly slap, feeble and weak. He had no idea who he was dealing with. I could take a lot more than that. I couldn't help it. I laughed. And he started cursing at me in anger, grabbing my shoulders and shaking me.

My friend's head suddenly popped up over the front seat of the car. "Hey!" she said. "Leave her alone!"

"The bitch bit me!" he said, drawing his hand back to slap me again.

"Do you know who her brother is?" His hand paused. He knew. "And you know who her cousins are?" He knew that, too. It was a small town, and my male relatives were not to be trifled with.

He leaned back, his anger somewhat in check. But his teen libido still wasn't quite in check. He reached across me and opened the door. "Fine. But you can either put out or get out."

And so I got out. And started walking down that tiny road between two swampy areas. Bullfrogs sang their throaty song, mocking my stupidity. I didn't care. "Fuck you, Jeremiah!" I screamed.

And then the car pulled up beside me and my friend pleaded with me to get in. "He won't touch you, I promise. I'm sorry."

I was so stubborn and angry, I would have kept walking. Except that I had no idea where I was. And so I got back into the car.

They wouldn't take me home. I guess they were afraid that my brother would come rushing out, ready to beat them up and defend his little sister's honor.

Instead, they took me to the town square and dumped me out. I walked the rest of the way home.

* * *

Twenty years later, I looked at Martin and realized that some men never grow up. Never trust a man with a pencil-thin moustache.

I got into my car and drove away, my mind churning over where I could go.

I could drive back to the truck stop and sleep in my car. But there were lots of people at truck stops. Especially men. And in my current state of mind, I just couldn't deal with that. I needed to find somewhere I felt safe, or I needed to find an all-night drugstore, buy a bunch of sleeping pills and get it all over with.

A few years ago, I read an article that said that once a person contemplates suicide, they are much more likely to attempt it in the future. It typically isn't something a person acts upon the first time it occurs to them. Instead, each time you think about it, consider it, the more it seems like a valid option. I thought about it that night. I thought seriously about it. I was worthless, after all. That's what my ex-husband had told me in one of our just-before-divorce arguments. People say things in anger all the time. I'm sure I said things, too. But some things stick more than others. And that word "worthless" stuck in my head for years. In fact, it's still there.

But I wouldn't go for the pills that night. Because another thought entered my head. A place where I might not get turned away. A place where I'd be safe.

And that's when I decided to drive to Rock House. Because that's where my rock was.

* * *

And that was the beginning of my short period of homelessness.

I would get a few hours of sleep in Aries' stall at night, and then I'd drive to the truck stop, wash up, change my clothes and go to work.

If anyone knew about it, no one ever let on. Nobody ever commented that I smelled peculiar, either, although I'm pretty sure I did. In fact, I probably reeked. I can't say that I experienced the homelessness of sleeping on a street corner and panhandling for money. But I washed my hair in the sink of the truck stop bathroom, using the hand soap from the dispenser. And I'll never forget that feeling of uncertainty, the fear that my children and I would never be together again. But I went to work and I smiled and I didn't share my predicament with another soul. Sharing hadn't worked out so well for me.

And then it was over and the kids and I had our home back. My brother and his girlfriend got back together and they moved away to another state and we moved back into the rental house. I was on my own and I swore I would never be that dependent on anyone again. I didn't care how hard I had to work.

12 Darkness

I was so wrapped up in working, determined to keep a roof over our heads, that important stuff was falling by the wayside. Important stuff like being an involved mother.

I would often come home at night to find a note that Joey had written me on my pillow. A note telling me how his day had been, or something he was particularly excited about. Or a note that would say, "Mom, please wake me up. I have something important to tell you."

I didn't know what else to do, but keep working and working. I was terrified of ending up on the street. Of being separated from my children. I just thought that the more I worked, the better things would be. I remember Joey literally getting on his knees and wrapping his arms around my legs, begging me to stay home. To spend one night just hanging out with him. And I would extricate his arms as gently as possible and try to explain how important it was that I work.

The girls had benefited from having me during their early childhood. They'd had me and the horses to guide them and form them and keep them busy and grounded. Joey had no such guidance or support. I did my best of course. I signed him up for Little League, and tried to get him to most of the games and practices. Often, however, I would end up sleeping in the car during his games, because I was simply so exhausted, I had to grab a bit of sleep whenever I could.

I was acutely aware that most of the other parents had a dim view of my parenting skills. Once, they had a bake sale to raise money for some of the extras our registration fees didn't cover. I had to work the day of the sale, but I wanted to contribute, so I came home from Shoney's at 3 a.m. (we closed at 2 a.m. on Fridays and Saturdays) and baked cupcakes to take to the bake sale. Unfortunately, because of the time it took to bake the cupcakes, I overslept the next morning and didn't have time to take them to the field before I had to be at work. Joey and Shannon were ok with it, because they got to eat the cupcakes. However, after the next practice, Joey handed me a note in a sealed envelope.

The note was signed by the "team moms" and was written to remind me of my duties as a responsible parent. It wasn't fair for some parents to bake and work at the bake sale, while others simply decided to shirk their parental responsibilities. So they had decided that I should pay an additional fee, to make up for my lack of support. The note was snarky and mean, and I tried not to let it bother me. But it did. It ate at me for years. And like a person with a sore who can't stop picking at it, I saved the letter and would sometimes pull it out of my junk drawer and read it, getting angry all over again.

Everything seemed bleak. We were unable to adequately care for Pibb's navicular and had found him a new home as a companion horse. We also had to find a new home for Ebony. Khan was sold to a concert violinist named Daniel Heifetz. Katie told me that Heifetz would go out to the pasture and play his violin for the horses. I used to imagine Khan, out there on a beautiful farm, listening to soothing music and being happy and cared for by the high-class people he was intended for.

And then the most cruel blow of all came. I was at home, between jobs, trying to get a little bit of sleep as usual, when Katie came in and shook me gently.

"Mom?" she said hesitantly. "I need you to wake up for a minute. I have something important to tell you."

She had sold Aries. We had talked about it, of course. There just wasn't enough money to care for the horses, and they had gone, one by one. Only Aries was left. And now even he was gone.

I didn't handle it well. Something snapped inside me. Something big. I raged. I threw things. God knows how much stuff I broke. I screamed. I cried. I begged. "Please, no," I said. "Please get him back."

"But Mom, you never even see him anymore." Now Katie was crying too. "And we just don't have the money to take care of him. He's better off with these people. They'll take good care of him."

"I'll take good care of him! I'll get another job!"

"Mom, you can't. You're already working all the time."

"I can. I can. I'll get a breakfast job. I have a lunch job and a dinner job. I'll get a breakfast job."

"And when will you sleep?"

"I don't need to sleep! I need Aries!" I was wailing like a three-year-old child. I was being unreasonable and petulant and I knew it. It was true. I hadn't even seen Aries in a long time, and I knew Katie was thinking of selling him, but when it actually happened, I couldn't take it. It was like everything in my life was suddenly bad. Like a grey screen had been pulled down in front of my eyes, dimming all the colors and draining any happiness or joy out of my life.

To this day, I am ashamed of that tirade. Of how it must have made Katie feel. Of how selfish I was. But I can't take it back, and I hope that she has forgiven me.

I think that was the start of the real darkness. My sleep deprivation caused me to have hallucinations. I vividly remember seeing a wolf running alongside my car on my way home one night. A wolf with glowing red eyes and long saber tooth tiger-like fangs. A wolf who could run 60 miles an hour. At the time, it seemed so real and terrifying. And there was the night I came home, exhausted as usual, and needing to sleep, but instead I sat in a corner of my kitchen with a baseball bat in my hands, because I was convinced someone was going to try to break in and hurt my children.

It was a constant struggle not to give in to that darkness, as anyone with severe depression can tell you. And those thoughts that began weeks before kept popping up. Kept invading my brain. But I had to keep going for my kids. And for Aries.

Because I looked at my life and knew that I couldn't simply wait tables and work 15 hour days, seven days a week for the rest of my life. I wanted more and I had to have a plan. I had to get Aries back.

I started looking at the other women I worked with. Ones who only worked one job and drove nice cars and weren't perpetually exhausted. I started asking them questions about how they did it. At first, I got some bits of sanctimonious advice, but when I kept digging, I found out more.

Many of them were married, and only worked to have spending money. So, option 1: Find a husband, preferably a rich one. One who loved animals and could afford a large ranch with plenty of room for horses. But I wasn't interested in husband-hunting. I wasn't particularly interested in men at all, for the time being.

Some of the servers were married or not, but were also on assistance. Option 2: That was a short-term option, and I was looking for a long-term option.

Option three involved Wendy. Wendy wasn't married, had two kids, lived in a nice apartment, had nice things, and didn't seem to struggle like I did. While she did work two jobs, she didn't work nearly the hours I did and always seemed to have money and plenty of leisure time. And she had horses.

Some time after that night, when she sent me home with Martin, I finally discovered Wendy's secret. Wendy was a kept woman. She was involved with a married man who paid her rent, bought her groceries, bought her truck, and gave her expensive jewelry. I was fascinated by Wendy. She was a little on the wild side, a free spirit, who didn't much care what anyone else thought of her. Pretty much my complete opposite.

Wendy typically spent her time with older men, ones who had enough money to buy her things. She would also see other men besides her married fellow. In the early days of cell phones, when they were still *very* expensive, her benefactor got her a cell phone because he was worried about her driving home alone late at night. He paid the bill every month, of course. But she had spent a lot of time talking to another man on the cell phone, running up the bill. She showed the bill to the other man, and told him she just didn't have the money to pay for it. So he gave her the money, which she pocketed. She got a free cell phone, and made money off it! Whatever Wendy wanted, she figured out a way to get, no matter what.

Some people would judge Wendy's behavior harshly. Some people would have a word for what Wendy did. And sometimes, I would even feel a little sorry for the men she used. But then again, they were using her too. They got what they wanted. She got what she wanted. So which one of them was the victim?

I used to watch the way Wendy talked to men, how she flattered them and deferred to them. Sometimes she would act as if she didn't have a thought in her head, and would let them patiently explain things to her ... about topics on which I knew she was completely well educated. And they loved it. She was very clever, and I knew that if she were in my shoes, she'd have figured out how to convince a man to buy Aries back for her. In fact, she did that very thing with a colt that she had sold and then decided she wanted back.

And yet, I couldn't be like Wendy. I just didn't have it in me. So option three also wasn't a valid option. I had to figure out my own option.

So one day, I drove myself to Clayton State University, applied for student aid, and enrolled myself in college.

I would never have considered going to college, if it weren't for being so desperate to get Aries back. Although I was always a straight A student in school, I hadn't even finished the 10th grade. When the girls were little, I had taken the test to get my GED, and I had even taken the SAT. I had always been good at taking tests.

However, walking between all those stately brick buildings made my knees shake a little. Everything and everyone looked so ... collegiate. My plan was to enroll as a business major. It seemed the safest course of action to get me the kind of money I needed to be a wealthy horse owner. I could envision myself wearing sharp business suits to work, and then driving home down a long driveway to my stately mansion fit for a CEO. And I could see Aries, presiding over my elegant stables that held all the horses we'd lost and others besides.

Of course, my plan wasn't the same as my dream. My dream was to be a writer and live in the middle of nowhere and wear boots and jeans and ball caps every day. I would still have a long driveway, because I like my privacy. I would be a hermit if life would allow it. But I would like to walk down that driveway every day and put manuscripts in the mailbox and take royalty checks out.

My experience with the *Horse Illustrated* article I had written about Shannon and Pibb had whetted my appetite for that dream. But my practical side, and the advice of everyone who wanted to give me advice, said that that wasn't a solid option. And if I was to get Aries back, I needed solid. I needed safe. I needed a sure thing.

13 PLAN

MY sure thing sure was tough to find time for. I had to keep both jobs, so working time in to attend college classes at night was a challenge. Finding time to complete the coursework was even tougher. I drove with an open textbook on the car seat beside me, so I could read at stoplights.

And I still felt a little out of place. Although Clayton State catered to non-traditional students like me, I was still much older than most of the students. At first, I always sat in the back of the room and never spoke up in class. As a business major, I had to take classes like accounting and business math, but I also got to take ones I enjoyed more, like art appreciation and English composition.

It was during one of those English Comp classes that the professor decided to play a word association game. He would say a word, and then people would raise their hands and tell him the first word that came to their minds. He did a couple of words, and I didn't say anything, as usual. Then he said, "Sunset," and I felt my hand shoot into the air. He called on me, and I said, "Rock House Ranch."

Everyone turned and looked at me. You could have heard the proverbial pin drop. Or crickets chirping. Clearly, I was supposed to have said, "red" or "orange" or "beautiful." But the first thing that popped into my head was the sunsets I'd seen at Rock House Ranch, gazing over at Butcher's Dairy Farm across the road. (I've always found it a bit ironic that a man named "Butcher" owned a dairy farm.) For me, nothing could rival the emotional satisfaction I got from watching those gold and crimson sunsets over a field of impossibly green grass, with black and white cows scattered around. Though I've never seen a sunset in Key West, or any of those other exotic locales known for their sunsets, I can't imagine they could top the sunsets I saw during the happiest times of my life.

But life was moving on. I could still go to Rock House, although it wasn't the same without Aries there, so I didn't go as often as I used to. I did see him from time to time. His new owners boarded him at a farm where Katie worked, so sometimes I went there to pick her up. At first, he would see my car and come running up to the fence. I had to avert my eyes and force myself to drive past him. After a while, he would just lift his head to look at my car, and then of course, the day came that I pulled into the driveway, and he didn't even look up from his grazing.

But I had to push that to the back of my mind and focus on my classes, because that was the plan, and I had to stick to the plan.

It actually helped that I was so busy, so I tried to cram as much into each day as possible. I had lost even more weight and was in the best physical shape of my life. Walking had turned into running, and Joey often went with me on my runs, riding his bicycle beside me.

Joey was still playing baseball and Shannon was still competing in Special Olympics. Although she wasn't riding anymore, she participated in other sports, including swimming and track and field events.

And of course, my college classes were a major focus. I enjoyed learning new things and every class I got under my belt was one step closer to my goal. It was just like losing weight... one step at a time. Like that song from *Rudolph the Red-Nosed Reindeer*, I just had to put one foot in front of the other, until I could walk out the door ... degree in hand and fabulous career in front of me.

I was still working at Shoney's and C and D's, and going to school, but it wasn't long before I added a third job to my already-full plate.

I saw a tiny advertisement in the local paper for a writer, so I went in to fill out the application. The process ended up taking over two hours, because the company, FC&A, required a battery of tests ... personality test, IQ test, honesty test, etc.

A few days later, I got a form rejection notice in the mail. "Thank you for applying, blah, blah, blah." And then I did something I thought was totally out of character for me. I refused to give up.

I called the company and spoke to Barbara, the receptionist. She was extremely kind and helpful. I asked her what type of books the company published, and she said primarily self-help health books.

I asked if I could bring some writing samples by. She said I could. However, the only published sample I had was the *Horse Illustrated* article about Shannon and Mr. Pibb. I'd won some writing contests and had some things published when I was in middle school and high school, but I'd long since lost track of them ... not that they'd have been appropriate anyway.

So I wrote something. I went to the library at Clayton State, did some research, and wrote an article about cluster headaches.

The following day, I took Barbara that article, the *Horse Illustrated* article, and a paper I'd written for biology class. My assignment had been to trace the path of a molecule of O_2 from the moment it entered the body, thorough its conversion to H_2O. I figured the professor had to read hundreds of those papers, and most were probably dry as a bone. So I personified my O_2 molecule. It became Oscar and Otis, twin atoms joined at the hip by a double covalent bond. Otis was always freaking out about what was happening to them ... one moment they were drifting happily along through the atmosphere, and the next, they were sucked into this huge nasal structure. Oscar patiently explained the whole process to his brother until they encountered Hillary and Heather, two hydrogen atoms that Oscar bonded with to form my requisite molecule of H_2O. Otis, however, refused to bond with hydrogen sisters Hilda and Helga. Instead, he went screaming off into the body somewhere to become an "oxygen free radical." It was borderline inappropriate for my biology class and wildly inappropriate as a writing sample for a publishing company. But I didn't really know that.

And yet, the very next day, I got a phone call. The manager of the editorial department at FC&A offered me a freelance assignment, and soon, I was freelancing for them on a regular basis. I was working, study-ing, writing, parenting, and working some more. Life was busy indeed.

I hadn't lost sight of the plan, but you know what they say about the best-laid plans of mice and men. Or horses and women.

14 RETURN OF THE KING

Like many low-income Americans, I have always had a love/hate relationship with my vehicles. I had to depend on them to get me to work, but I never had the money to buy a new car, so I drove a never-ending chain of clunkers. My ex-husband was handy with a wrench and socket, having tinkered on dozens of hot rods in the late sixties and early seventies. So when I was married, I could always depend on him to keep our cars going.

After my divorce, however, I had no one to take care of those tasks for me. And most professional mechanics would charge me an arm and a leg for the simplest of repairs. So sometimes I had to improvise. I became quite proficient at changing tires, since I refused to buy new tires at all, choosing instead to wait until a tire blew out and was completely beyond repair before replacing it ... with a used tire. I changed tires in all kinds of terrain, and in all kinds of weather. It was rare for anyone to offer to assist me.

Once, the fuel pump went out on the Ford Tempo I was driving. Luckily, a friend of ours knew a mechanic who owed him a favor, so on a sunny Saturday, he brought the mechanic to my house to replace my fuel pump. When they arrived, it was clear to me that the mechanic wasn't happy to be there. His expression was surly and he answered all my questions with a combination of grunts and monosyllabic words. But my friend assured me that he was a great mechanic and that replacing the fuel pump would take him no time at all. My friend left, and since the mechanic clearly didn't want me around, I excused myself and went inside to try to get a couple hours sleep before work.

When I woke up, the mechanic was gone. He had replaced the old fuel pump with a new one. The only catch was that the fuel pump was located inside the fuel *tank*. And he hadn't bothered putting the fuel tank back into my car. The tank was just sitting on my carport floor, with bolts and debris scattered all around.

I didn't know what to do. I had to be at work by 5. I never missed work. That wasn't part of the plan. And obviously, I couldn't drive the car without a fuel tank.

So I decided I could do it myself.

The tank was large and rather heavy, but I managed to slide it underneath the car. Then I just had to figure out how to lift it up by myself and get it all hooked up and bolted back in. I found some pieces of wood in my carport and lifted one side of the tank up, shoving the pieces of wood underneath it. Then I would go to the other side, lift it up a little, and slide some pieces of wood underneath it. I went back and forth, lifting each side up a little more each time, until I had it up high enough to get my jack underneath it. I jacked up the one side, and then found a concrete block to put under it to hold it up. Then I took the jack to the other side and repeated the process.

Now I had the fuel tank up high enough for me to crawl under it. I just had to figure out how to reconnect the fuel lines and electrical wires and bolt it back into place.

Years later, I would find a wonderful mechanic named Greg. He was my dad's neighbor and was a whiz at fixing my bevy of rattletrap cars. And he never overcharged me. I appreciated Greg more than he ever knew. I wish I had told him. Because one day, Greg was changing out a fuel tank in a car, and a stray spark or static electricity or something ignited some fumes and caught Greg on fire. He was burned from head to toe and passed away a couple of days later at Grady Hospital in Atlanta.

And Greg was a savvy mechanic who knew what he was doing. I was a middle-aged waitress who didn't have a clue. Or even an instruction manual.

But I guess God does protect children and fools, because miraculously, I figured out how everything attached and got the fuel tank hooked up and bolted in and I still had time to take a shower before work.

But my car problems did bring some good things into my life.

* * *

My civics class was an easy A. We spent more time socializing and talking about current events than we did studying. And so I became a little more engaged with those class members than I usually did.

One night after class, I was walking to my car, but I paused to watch a pickup basketball game some of my classmates had started. The ball rolled toward me and so I picked it up and two-handed it back to one of the players.

"Oho!" he said. "Looks like blondie knows how to play ball."

He heaved the ball back to me. "Go ahead, slim. Show us what you can do."

I turned and took a shot at the basket. I had a backpack full of books and a purse on my arm, so it wasn't the most graceful of shots, but it went in the basket and that's all that counts.

"All right!" he said. "Legs is on my team."

And I put my purse and backpack on a bench and joined in the game. I was probably quite a sight, a middle-aged woman in a short skirt, playing basketball with a bunch of twenty-something guys in the dark, but it was more fun than I'd had in a long time.

The guy who had invited me to play was in my class, but he didn't seem to know my name. Instead, throughout the game, he called me "blondie" and "legs" and "slim."

After an hour or so, I realized that I had to get home, since I needed to be up early in the morning. I excused myself and left them all still at the goal and walked alone to my car.

I got in my good old clunker and it cranked right up. There was a slight problem, however. When I turned my lights on, nothing happened. My dashboard lights weren't working either. And it was too dark and too late to fiddle around with it to figure out what was wrong.

I got out of the car with my purse and backpack and headed back towards the buildings, thinking I'd find a payphone and call someone to come get me.

On the way there, however, I ran into a couple of the guys I'd been playing ball with … one of them the one who'd invited me into the game.

"What's up, slim?" he asked. "Coming back for more?"

I explained my problem, and he offered to drive me home. I thought about how long I'd have to wait for anyone to come pick me up, and decided to take him up on his kind offer.

We walked together to his little black sports car. There were books and other stuff piled high in the passenger seat. I was surprised to find that I thought this was a good sign. No girlfriend in the picture, or the seat would be clear.

My house was about 45 minutes from the campus, and the first part of the drive was a little quiet and awkward. I asked him where he lived, and when he told me, I realized that he lived the opposite direction from the campus that I did. Taking me home was costing him more than two hours of his time.

"I'm so sorry," I said. "I didn't realize…"

"No sweat, slim," he said. "I never sleep anyway."

"Neither do I," I said, "But not from choice."

And so I started talking about my life to this almost-stranger. And discovered that he was funny and kind and smart and understanding.

He told me about his prosthetic eye. He'd fallen on an ice pick when he was only five years old. Horrifying as that sounded, he made light of it. He was a computer guy in the still-early days of computing, and he was the only boy in a family of five sisters.

And I told him about Aries. I told him how I'd once been privileged with the company of the most beautiful horse in the world. I told him that was why I was going to college at my age. I told him how determined

I was to get him back, and that when that happened, Aries and I were going to grow old and toothless together.

When we arrived at my house, I didn't want to stop talking to him. But it was late, and he still had to drive all the way back. So I decided to have a pre-final study session at my house and I invited him. I invited other people from our class as well, but only he and a friend of his showed up. And after that night, Sam and I were pretty much inseparable.

There were obstacles to our relationship, of course. There was the fact that I was twelve years his senior, but I'd never been one to let societal norms stand in my way. And there was the fact that he was raised in an extremely conservative Christian family – a family that disapproved of me intensely – to the point that Sam would not take me to his parent's house. And of course, there was the fact that I had three kids – a fact that had discouraged many a potential suitor. But I was head over heels in love, and it seemed to me to be reciprocated.

Sam was intensely interested in astronomy, and had a super-duper telescope that he would set up in his backyard. So I took him to Rock House and had him set up his telescope in the pasture one night. He was thrilled with the view he got without all the streetlights to interfere with the view. I preferred viewing the stars without mechanical assistance. I just sat on a blanket on the ground and drank them in.

As much as I loved Sam, however, my happiness wasn't complete without Aries. I was still trying to save money, still taking classes, but it seemed that every time I would get a little money set aside, my car would break down, or one of the kids would need something.

It was discouraging, and his owners had moved him to a different farm, so I didn't even get to see him anymore. And without Katie there to keep an eye on him, I worried about him. I used to drive past the farm where he was (or at least where I thought he was) and I would slow down and crane my neck, trying to see if I could catch a glimpse of him. I wondered if he was all right. Was he being fed properly? Chow-hound that he was, he still had a tendency to drop weight quickly. Were they keeping an eye out for colic? For some reason, Aries was predisposed to mild colic, but it could turn into a major problem if you didn't spot it early. The symptoms were subtle, but I could tell just by looking at his face. Were his new owners that vigilant? Would they miss the signs until it turned into a fatal episode?

I thought about turning down the driveway and just asking to see him, but how would I explain that I was stalking my former horse? How weird is that?

So I tried to occupy my mind by staying as busy as possible. For once, exhaustion was my friend.

One day, I was (as usual) trying to catch a little bit of sleep before going to work when the phone rang. It was Katie. She was working at Rock House again, and she said they had just gotten a new horse in. She said that he looked familiar, and she wanted me to come and see if I recognized him. I hesitated. I was so tired, facing a long night at work, and a couple hours of shut-eye sure would help. But something in her tone convinced me, so I dragged my droopy self to the car.

Horses changed hands a lot, and it wasn't unusual for us to run across a horse we had known in previous years. Usually, it had new owners and a new name, but it was always a little thrill ... like running into an old friend at the mall.

I pulled into the driveway at Rock House, and Katie met me at the car. She seemed nervous for some reason as she led me into one of the new barns they had recently built. "He's down here, in the last stall on the left." She stopped part-way down the aisle, and I walked ahead. Through the bars of the stall, I saw a beautiful gray horse munching on some hay. I felt tears begin to sting my eyes. He lifted his head and looked at me, and then nickered softly. I couldn't say anything, because of the grapefruit-sized lump in my throat.

"Mom?" Katie was concerned that I hadn't said anything. "You know who it is, don't you?"

I nodded. I knew.

"Happy Mother's Day," she said. She lifted a gleaming leather halter off a hook on his stall door and swung the door open. It was then I noticed the brass name plate beside the door, and a matching one on the halter. They both read "Aries."

I slid his halter on him, and Katie and I walked him to the pasture gate. I took his halter off and let him go. As he cantered away, Katie said, "He's home now, and he's never going to leave you again."

And just like that, my plan was superseded by my wonderful, resourceful daughter.

Katie had heard that Aries' owners were trying to sell him. The girl they'd bought him for had lost interest in horses. Katie knew that if they sold him, we might never be able to find him again, so she came up with the money to buy him back for me.

She had arranged for Aries to board for free, as part of her salary. She also planned to give lessons on him, so he could earn his keep.

But the first lesson she was going to give on him belonged to me.

15 CHANGES

THE next day, I arrived for my first lesson, nervous as a long-tailed cat in a room full of rocking chairs.

It wasn't going to be the first time I had been on Aries.

* * *

It happened when I was still married, before the madness of working all the time. I had walked and walked and struggled and sacrificed. Given up pizza. And ice cream. And I had lost 75 pounds. At the time, it seemed like a lot, although by the end, I would have lost over 150 pounds.

But at the time, I had lost 75. And I thought that maybe that was enough. Maybe, I could rush my dream just a little and ride Aries.

I waited until no one was around of course. I tacked him up and I led him to the mounting block. I made sure his girth was extra tight. I closed my eyes and took a deep breath. Then I put my foot in the stirrup and swung my still-heavy thigh across his back and plunked down. He didn't budge.

We just stood there for a moment. I was thrilled. I gave him a little kick and asked him to walk. He walked. I was *riding*. I was riding *Aries*. Suddenly, I wasn't just thrilled, I was downright giddy. My dreams were coming true. My hard work was paying off. I was just like Elizabeth Taylor in *National Velvet*.

And then he bucked me off.

I was shocked and confused. It seemed to take forever, that trip to the ground, that sudden what-the-hell-just-happened descent. The impact to my body was jarring, knocking the breath out of me. The impact to my ego, to my silly day-dreaming brain was much worse. I had never seen Aries buck anyone off. And he decided to dump *me*? Me. The one who loved him more than anything in the world. I was so hurt, I just lay there in the damp grass, feeling sorry for myself.

Aries stood just a few feet away, grazing nonchalantly. He wasn't trying to run away, so I just continued to lie there, processing my epic failure.

And then he noticed that I hadn't gotten up. He lifted his head and nickered at me. Not a gentle, "Hey, how ya doin'? Sorry I just dumped you" nicker, but a deep insistent, "What the hell ya doin' laying there like a loser? Get up already."

And still I laid there. So Aries walked over to me and nudged me with his muzzle, like a dam encouraging her newborn foal to its feet for the first time.

And still I laid there, although a smile was creeping its way onto my lips.

Aries snorted. And nudged me again. Much harder this time. So hard, he practically rolled me onto my side. I started laughing and I sat up, cross-legged in the grass, one side of my face plastered with dirt mixed with dew.

Aries seemed satisfied that I was in an upright position, and went back to grazing.

And I knew that he didn't dump me because he didn't love me. He dumped me because I was fat and clumsy and didn't know what I was doing. It wasn't time yet. I thought I had time. I could be patient.

But then I got so busy working, I didn't have time. And then he was gone.

* * *

But the day had finally arrived. I was going to ride Aries. And everything was different now. Because he was *my* horse. Not just in spirit. Not just in my head. Mine. Katie had given him to me. Officially. I was the rightful owner of the most beautiful horse in the world, and I was going to ride him.

I tacked him up in the wash rack and followed Katie to the arena. I stared hard at the mounting block as we strolled past it. Katie didn't give it so much as a sideways glance. She just kept walking.

On the way to the riding arena, we passed the dressage arena. It was bounded by railroad ties. They weren't as tall as a mounting block, but they'd give me a little bit of a lift. Katie ignored that as well, although she probably noticed my longing gaze toward their solid presence.

We entered the arena, shutting the gate behind us. We walked to the middle, and Katie turned to me. "Grab a handful of mane," she advised. I had a quick flashback to the last time I tried to mount a horse from the ground. A knot of anxiety formed in my stomach, but Katie was a no-nonsense kind of person, and at that point, she was not my daughter. She was my riding instructor, and I was not going to argue with her.

I reached up and grabbed a hunk of mane with my left hand and the back of the saddle with my right. I lifted my left leg up and inserted my toe into the stirrup iron, astonished at how easy it seemed now. I took a deep breath and pushed off with my right leg, swinging it up and over his hindquarters.

"Now, don't plop down on his back," Katie admonished.

I was surprised to find that I could hold myself above his body with just one leg in the stirrup. I settled myself slowly and carefully onto Aries' back and found my other stirrup with my toe.

* * *

Years before, I had received tickets to see *Cats* at the Fox Theatre in Atlanta. I was excited, but I had no idea what to wear. I never bought clothes for myself. Shopping for clothes in my size was not a pleasure and I just couldn't bring myself to spend the money when the kids needed so much. So my sister sent me an outfit. A loaner dress that would be appropriate to wear to the glitzy Fox.

My husband took me, and I marveled at all the people, many of them dressed in evening wear ... men in tuxedos and women in evening gowns, dripping with jewels. The Fox had only recently been rescued from demolition and restored to its former glory thanks to a huge grassroots fund raising campaign. This was where *Gone With the Wind* had premiered in 1939. Clark Gable and Vivien Leigh once walked the lobby. Margaret Mitchell most certainly had been here.

Not everyone was dressed like they just stepped out of a James Bond movie, but they seemed to be the only ones I noticed. The beautiful, the slender, the rich, the educated. And enormous me in a borrowed dress. My husband, on the other hand, was trim and handsome, muscles honed by years of carpenter work and hours spent in the gym. He was probably wearing jeans, but he could pull that off, and he didn't really care what people thought of him anyway.

We went into the auditorium and I was awestruck by the stars painted on the ceiling, mimicking an outdoor sky.

And then we went to take our seats, and my nervous awe turned to full-blown panic. The seats weren't built to accommodate 300-pound farm girls from Arkansas. I was *not* Vivien Leigh. I twisted myself sideways a little and managed to wedge myself into the seat. It wasn't comfortable, but I breathed a sigh of relief. I was about to see a legendary musical.

I was enthralled by the costumes and the music. My husband was not. After a long day at work, he wasn't happy about being dragged into the city to watch a bunch of people dressed like cats sing and dance. He was sound asleep within minutes.

At intermission, people walked past us, looking curiously at the huge lady sitting sideways in her seat and the man sound asleep beside her, his mouth gaping open. When he let out a loud snore, I decided it was time to go home. He protested, but I insisted. I was uncomfortable and he was tired and we didn't belong there.

Several years later, I returned to the Fox Theatre to see *Cats* with Sam. I settled confidently into my seat, and realized that I had room beside me to put my purse. I was wearing a little black skirt, a green silk blouse and strappy 4-inch heels.... that all belonged to me. I was mesmerized by the entire show. While my body size did not define me ... does not define anyone ... it is amazing the difference a few pounds can make.

* * *

My first lesson on Aries was a resounding success. I walked, trotted and even cantered. Most importantly, I didn't hit the ground.

16 HAT TRICK

AFTER my first lesson, Katie continued coaching me. My lessons were a bit more informal than those of her paying clients. She would take me out to the arena, give me a couple of things she wanted me to work on, and turn me loose. She had confidence in my ability to follow directions and knew I was motivated to improve. I wasn't a teenager, after all.

I had sat through Lord knows how many riding lessons when the girls were growing up. I'd attended countless horse shows, hitching up a trailer at 3 or 4 in the morning to travel to various parts of the state and country. Katie had competed in almost every riding discipline, including English and Western pleasure, eventing, show jumping, barrel racing, and even driving.

Observing all this riding may have given me an intellectual edge when I finally began riding myself. However, watching it and doing it are entirely different. And doing it correctly is much more difficult than most people imagine.

In particular, I had trouble getting my diagonals. In hunt seat equitation, riders often post at the trot. This is called a "rising trot," because the rider rises up and down out of the saddle with the rhythm of the horse's trot. Your butt is supposed to be in the air when the horse's outside foreleg is in the air.

I knew the old rule "rise and fall with the outside wall," but I couldn't figure out how to actually do that. Katie told me to feel for it, because if you look down to see where the horse's legs are, you throw your center of gravity off and break your concentration.

I kept trying to feel for it, but just couldn't seem to figure it all out.

Katie knew how much I longed to get in the show ring and win those ribbons I dreamed about as a kid, so she was prepping me to enter a local "Britches and Boots" circuit. She also suggested a new show name for Aries that was perfect – Almost Goodbye.

My first show was going to be a "fun show" at Rock House, so at least I'd be on familiar territory, but I was beginning to get panicked about not being able to get my diagonals.

I expressed my fear to Sam, and he came up with a solution. When the announcer asked for a rising trot, I would begin to post, and I would look at Sam, who would be ringside. If I was on the incorrect diagonal, he would touch the brim of his hat. I would sit a beat, which would correct my mistake. Unless the judge was looking right at me when I picked up my trot, he or she would never even be aware of my mistake.

At the time, I never thought of it as cheating. It didn't seem any different than a coach giving instructions from the sidelines, the same as the crazy hand signals baseball managers came up with. But I didn't want anyone else to know about it. I didn't want anyone, particularly my daughter, to know that I hadn't mastered my diagonals.

My most salient memory of that first show was how dry my mouth became the second I entered the arena. I had never been fond of being in the spotlight, but that level of stage fright was new to me. I wasn't just afraid of embarrassing myself, but of letting Katie down. And Aries, who had grown accustomed to winning. And Sam, who was now my horse show partner in crime.

The hat trick worked beautifully (I think we won), and my first show season had begun. Sam became my patient show companion, traveling to each show, hanging out at the horse trailer, standing ringside to cheer me on and correct my diagonals. Throughout the spring and summer, we attended shows all over the area. Shannon and Joey tagged along, of course, and made friends wherever we went.

At one point, Katie decided to take me with her to a bigger show, at Chateau Elan. Chateau Elan was located north of Atlanta, in Braselton, Georgia. It was a winery and resort, but also had a horse show arena.

Aries and I would be competing in the adult beginner category, but the competition was much stiffer than the small shows I'd been attending on the south side of Atlanta. As usual, Sam came along and helped me out.

We entered every class in our division. After our competition was finished, Katie and her clients still had classes, so I untacked Aries, hosed him off and headed back to the trailer. The arena was down in sort of a small valley, and a steep trail led up to the parking area. As I was leading Aries up that trail, the announcer came over the loudspeaker to announce the winners of the adult beginner division.

Aries stopped dead in his tracks and lifted his head as if he was listening. I hadn't even realized that they were announcing our division, but apparently he had. And that's when I heard that Tammy Waldrop on Almost Goodbye had won Reserve Grand Champion.

Later, Katie and her students would tell me that they were watching us from the stands by the arena. They saw Aries stop and lift his head as the announcement was made. They watched as he listened and then, having heard our names, dropped his head back down and plodded forward, his day's work finished. They laughed and said, "It looked like he understood what was being said." I thought, "Of course he did!" But I didn't say that. I just laughed with them.

Afterward, Katie encouraged me to speak to the judge. I can't remember who she was, but apparently she was pretty well-known and respected in the hunter community. Katie said it was a golden opportunity to get a little feedback from someone of her stature.

So I screwed up my courage and approached her. I introduced myself, and she said she remembered me, and that I had a lovely horse. I asked her if she had any advice for me for improvement.

She looked directly at me with cool blue eyes and said, "Learn your diagonals."

I flushed and mumbled something, certain that she knew about my deception.

It seems so silly now that I had confided my problem with my diagonals to Sam, but hadn't shared my difficulty with the person who could help me most – Katie.

But at the next horse show we attended, she was giving me some last minute advice before we went into the arena, and I blurted out how worried I was about getting my diagonals.

"I think you're just rushing," she said. She'd been watching me, of course, so she knew that I always began posting as soon as they called for it. But she'd also seen me correcting my diagonal, which she thought I was doing completely on my own. "Take your time. You don't have to start posting the second they call for it. Make sure you wait until you feel his outside shoulder moving forward under the saddle, and then start posting."

They were calling for my class, so I had to ride away, but I had just experienced a "Eureka!" moment.

I had the best ride of my life thus far and won the class. When I rode out of the arena, Katie was beaming at me. "See! You didn't rush and you nailed your diagonals! That was amazing!"

I had to tell her that, while the not rushing advice helped, the real gem was the bit about feeling for his shoulder to move forward. "I never told you that before?" she asked.

"If you did, I wasn't listening," I said. Which was entirely possible. She would be giving me instructions, but I would be concentrating so hard on riding, I would only hear about half of what she said. So while I remembered hearing her tell me to feel for my diagonals, I didn't remember her telling me exactly what I was feeling *for*. Once I knew to pay attention to the motion of Aries' shoulder, I had it.

We still had more than half the show season to go and we breezed along, winning almost every class. I did have some trouble at one show, and learned yet another valuable lesson from my daughter.

The night before the show, we'd had heavy rain, and mud and puddles were everywhere – including the arena. One end of the arena looked like a small lake. They tried to drain as much of it as they could, but there was still a large body of standing water in one corner.

Aries loved to roll in the mud. Stepping in the mud was another story. We were approaching the huge puddle just when they called for a canter.

Aries picked up his canter, but bent his body to avoid the water and ended up on the wrong lead. That had never happened before. I pulled him back down and started over on the correct lead and we finished the class. I can't remember how we placed, but I remember Katie was not happy with me. But not because of how I placed.

She told me that after we missed that lead, that my entire body language changed. "Your shoulders slumped, your facial expression changed, you lowered your head. You looked defeated. NEVER look defeated. I don't care what happens in there. You keep going and you keep a smile on your face. Never let them see you sweat!"

She was right, of course. And she practiced what she preached.

* * *

In show jumping, there is a set course that you have to jump in a certain order. But there are different patterns for different divisions.

If you go over the wrong jump on the course, you are instantly disqualified. The announcer will come over the loudspeaker and say something like, "Number 32, you are off course and may exit the arena." It made sense from a time standpoint, as there wasn't any point in wasting time finishing the course if you're disqualified. I always thought it was a little embarrassing for the rider, though.

At one particular show I remember, Katie had taken several students and spent a lot of time making sure they had memorized their courses. So much time, in fact, that she didn't have time to concentrate on her own class and she forgot her pattern.

She knew she was off course after the first jump. But she didn't hear the announcement to exit, so she kept going. She finished the entire course and left the arena. A few moments later, the announcement came, delayed though it was. She was disqualified.

After the show, however, the judge came to find Katie. She told her that if she hadn't been off course, she most definitely would have won the class. And she explained that, when Katie started jumping, she did it with such confidence, that she made the judge think that perhaps *she* didn't know the correct course. That's why she didn't have them interrupt Katie. She let her finish the course and then consulted her paperwork to make sure she wasn't mistaken about which course Katie should have been jumping. It was a huge compliment, and I was so proud of her. I just needed to learn how to be more like my daughter sometimes.

* * *

At the end of the show season, there was an awards dinner. Aries and I took home a couple of year-end awards, although mostly because there were only a few people who had made it to all the shows. Still, it was a wonderful evening and very satisfying. And I still cherish those ribbons.

17 ROCK HOUSE

As much as I enjoyed showing Aries, as proud as I was to have those ribbons and trophies, my happiest days were still at Rock House Ranch, just going on trail rides and grooming him, relaxing and hanging out.

Sam had always been a "city boy," so life at the ranch was new to him, but soon he was wearing boots and ball caps and going on trail rides with me. Once we startled up a pack of coyotes in the pasture. Sam hadn't believed that we even had coyotes in Georgia. He thought they were all out west somewhere, but there they were, leaping and darting every which way in front of us.

Aries presided over the Rock as if he owned the place. He was a favorite among Katie's students and his mischievous nature entertained everyone. He had long been an escape artist, constantly figuring out new ways to escape his stall or pasture. When he began escaping from his stall, and then letting other horses out, however, he went a little too far, and we added an extra latch to his door.

He was also intensely curious. Sam was into remote control vehicles, and took his RC car out to Rock House, where there was ample space to maneuver it. He found out that the horses weren't crazy about an electronic gizmo zipping around their pasture, and got a lot of amusement out of "herding" them with it. What he found even more amusing was the fact that all the other horses would run from his car, but as soon as they'd put it a safe distance away, they'd just stop, drop their heads and start grazing again as if nothing had happened. But not Aries. His curiosity would overrule his fear every time, and he just had to come back to that strange object and sniff at it. Sam would let the car sit there idling until Aries got up the courage to put his nose down to it, and then he would rev it just a bit and watch Aries jump back. And come back for more.

Aries' intelligence and his affinity for humans continued to set him apart from the other horses. Once, someone's truck broke down in the pasture. As men are wont to do whenever they see a raised hood on a vehicle, several guys gathered around, all staring at the engine and offering their opinions on what the problem might be. Aries sauntered over, pushed his way through the crowd, and stuck his head under the hood. If he had the power of speech, I swear he'd have said something like, "Well, boys, there's your problem right there. Look at those battery cables. No wonder she won't start."

We had to be careful that his curiosity and resourcefulness didn't get him in trouble, however. All the boarders at Rock House at the time kept their feed in barrels with lids that screwed on. This was to prevent any wayward horse, or one that liked to escape from his stall in the middle of the night, from getting into a feed barrel and eating too much, causing a potentially deadly colic episode. The screw-on lids were supposed to be horse proof, and they worked great. Until one day …

When it was time to turn the horses out to pasture, we would just open the stall doors and they would go. Any stragglers would be encouraged in the right direction by Cowdog, an Australian Cattle Dog that belonged to Chris and Mona, the owners of Rock House. Sometimes Hooch tried to help, too, but he hadn't had any formal herding training. His instincts were there, but his technique wasn't close to Cowdog's abilities.

But this particular day, Aries lagged behind when we opened all the doors, because he had his eye on one of those feed barrels. I had one of the other horses on the wash rack, so I was watching him. He nosed at the lid, but it didn't come off. So he picked it up with his teeth. There wasn't much feed in it so it was relatively light, enabling him to lift it off the ground and give it a little shake. There was enough weight in it, however, to cause the bottom of the barrel to shift whenever he shook it, which made the lid rotate ever so slightly. Aries' eyes lit up with a "Eureka!" moment of his own. And I watched as he set the barrel back down, grasped the lid by the knobby edge, and rotated the lid off with his teeth. I was horrified and impressed at the same time.

People constantly debate on whether animals can understand our words. It is pretty well accepted that dogs can understand lots of words. Of course they read our inflections and our emotions and our body language, but they also understand specific words. Horses understand words the same way. They learn "walk," "trot," and "canter" pretty easily when combined with physical cues. Good horses soon don't even need the physical cues and will respond to the words themselves. But how do we know that they can't understand more? There's really no definitive way to prove or disprove it.

I often thought that Aries understood much more than people gave him credit for, and one day, he gave me hilarious proof.

We were getting ready for a horse show, and I had bought him new shipping bandages. They were a beautiful royal blue. I got him straight out of his stall, put him on the washrack and wrapped all of his legs myself. I wasn't the fastest wrapper around, so it took me a while. When I was finished, I stood back and admired my handiwork. I told him how handsome and classy he looked with those bright blue bandages against his white legs.

I led him out of the washrack toward the trailer. I hadn't considered, however, that I hadn't allowed him to pee before getting him out of his stall. He would never have peed in the washrack, especially with me squatted down beside him, wrapping his legs. But he had to pee. And when you gotta go...

And so he let go. And when that torrential stream hit the dirt, it began to splatter muddy drops of dirt mixed with urine onto his brand new, sparkling blue shipping bandages that I was so proud of.

I turned in horror and said, "No! Not on the new bandages!"

And Aries stopped, hiked one leg into the air, and peed like a dog at a fire hydrant. The stream of urine was directed away from my coveted wraps and he was still able to finish peeing.

I have never seen a horse do that before or since. And believe what you will, I know that, whether he understood my specific words or not, he knew what I was distressed about and he knew how to react.

* * *

Just when I thought my life couldn't get better, it did. And it happened thanks to an abscessed tooth and yet another clunker of a car.

I was still freelancing for FC&A, which was located in Peachtree City. I could have mailed my completed assignments in, but since it was so close, I preferred to drive there and take them in person. I had a couple of reasons for this.

The first reason was that I was obsessed with making my deadlines, and I didn't want a slow postal service to cause a submission to be late. My children will tell you that one of my favorite books is *Horton Hatches the Egg*, by Dr. Seuss. One of Horton's repeated quotes is "I meant what I said and I said what I meant. An elephant's faithful one hundred percent." I would tell them that if more people were like Horton, the world would be a better place. And I tried to role-model that for them. I was Horton.

The second reason was that I loved the people at FC&A. From Barbara at the front desk to everyone in the editorial department, every person there was so *nice*. While I was happy with my life at the time, it was still stressful and chaotic. I was always running, trying to squeeze in time for everything. When I walked into the editorial department, it was like a little oasis of calm. Everything was so quiet, compared to the noisy environment I worked in. There was no music on the speakers, no clattering dishes, no chattering patrons, no arguing cooks, no dinging bell, no "order up!" Just calm, quiet, *nice* people working. When I visited the editorial department, I was like a kid with her nose pressed up against the glass of a candy shop.

And then I had an abscessed tooth. It wasn't the first time. Having no health insurance and not much money meant that I had learned to handle things on my own. Handling pain was a snap. I was used to that. I would lance the offending infected area with a needle and gargle with peroxide and wait for it to go away. But in the meantime, it looked terrible, which was a little embarrassing, but I had to just ignore that and wait for the swelling to go down.

I had an assignment due at FC&A that day, and I was on my way, when my car broke down. I couldn't get it started, and I was only a couple of miles away, so I figured I'd walk there, turn my assignment in, and ask if I could borrow their phone to call for help. It was spring in Georgia, which meant that it was sweltering hot. By the time I reached that air-conditioned haven, my hair was wet with sweat, straggling down beside my face, which was now beet red and of course, swollen up like I had an orange stuffed in my cheek.

I didn't realize what a sight I was until I knocked on the door of Camilla's office. She was the one I turned most of my assignments in to. Camilla is an extraordinarily empathetic person, and when she saw my face, shock and sympathy registered on her own face.

"Tammy!" she exclaimed. "What happened to you?"

The quietness of the office meant that everyone heard the alarm in her voice, and doors began to open and people came out, all of them concerned about me. It was a little overwhelming, and I was embarrassed. I explained what had happened and asked if I could borrow the phone.

Angela, the manager of the editorial department, asked if she could see me in her office. I was certain she was angry because I was causing a scene and disrupting the workflow.

That wasn't the case. Instead, when she shut the door to her office, she turned to me and said, "Why don't you want to work for us?"

I was confused. "I do work for you," I said.

"No, I mean, why don't you want to work for us full-time? Then you'd have health insurance."

My confusion turned to outright shock. "What are you talking about? I would LOVE to work here full time. You guys turned me down."

I explained to Angela about getting the rejection notice in the mail. She was unaware that I had even applied and said that she would check into it. She said that most people got rejected because of the assessments and she sent me on my way that day with a promise to check it out and let me know what she found out. She called me that night to tell me I had actually done well on all my assessments.

The tests weren't the issue. My lack of education and experience were an issue. Still, after interviews with Angela and the owner of the company, they offered me a full-time position. I was a full-time, professional writer. With health insurance.

In my interview with Angela, she was telling me all the amazing benefits FC&A offered their employees. The one thing that most people had a problem with, she said, was the vacation policy. You had to work for a whole year before you earned a week's paid vacation. She asked if I could live with that. I said I thought that I could, but what I was thinking was, "Are these people crazy? They get TWO days off every week!"

I quit both my serving jobs and became a member of the 9 to 5 set. In addition to weekends off, I also had several paid holidays. And paid sick days. And a 401k. And perhaps best of all, I no longer had to work on Thanksgiving, which quickly became my favorite day of the year, simply because I was so thankful that I didn't have to work.

18 ROCK BOTTOM

I couldn't sleep. I couldn't eat. I was a pathetic loser, and I couldn't seem to help myself.

My relationships with animals tend to be long-lasting. However, I've never been great at maintaining relationships with people. Specifically, with people of the opposite sex. But I thought that Sam was "the one." That he was different. That he really loved me and would never lie to me or cheat on me or betray me.

But it wasn't just that I had lost Sam. It was the fact that, if I couldn't make it work with Sam, whom I loved so passionately, I couldn't make it work with anyone. I was going to be alone forever.

I had a calendar on the wall of my office, and I would put a big red "X" across every day that I managed to go without calling his answering machine to hear his voice. Yes, I know. I've already admitted that I was pathetic.

A clean break would have been easier, but maybe Sam was having trouble letting go himself.

So we were trying to be friends, but just when I was getting better ... when I had several big red Xs all in a row on my calendar, he would call me. And it would all start again.

So one day, I came home to hear Sam's voice on *my* answering machine. I hadn't slept in several nights, and I was exhausted. But my stupid heart leapt at the sound of his voice. "Call me," he said.

I looked at the clock. He worked second shift, so that's where he would be. So I made an almost-fatal mistake. I called him at work. Someone else answered, and when I asked for Sam, they knew it was the *old* girlfriend calling, not the new one. Not the young one. Not the one that went home with him to meet his parents, whom I had never met, because they disapproved of me. So whoever answered the phone gave Sam a hard time. And when he came to the phone, he was angry. Why was I calling him at work? He didn't mean for me to call him *at work*. I thought it might be important. I thought maybe he needed me. I tried not to cry. I tried to be a grownup. But I failed. And he hung up.

I was so tired. That's not an excuse. There is no excuse. But I hadn't slept, and my brain wasn't working well. I just wanted to go to sleep and not care anymore. I was tired. I was tired of working and worrying and struggling and caring so much. About everybody. About everything. I was tired of everything being so freaking hard.

I had tried taking over-the-counter sleeping pills when my thoughts wouldn't let me rest. But they made my skin feel crawly and didn't help me sleep. So that's why there were two bottles of those sleeping pills in my kitchen cabinet. And they were right in front of my face. And before I knew it, I had swallowed them. All of them.

And then the phone rang again. It was Sam. Again.

"I'm sorry," he said. "I didn't mean to upset you. Maybe it would be best if we just didn't talk for a while."

And I laughed. I imagine it was one of those maniacal cartoon-like laughs. Because that was kind of how I was feeling. And Sam got worried. So he hung up and the phone rang again. This time it was Katie. Sam had called her at work and made her promise to go check on me. When I heard Katie's voice, the reality of what I had done hit me. Was I *crazy*? Well, yes.

I didn't want to alarm her, but I couldn't think of what to do. Could I make myself vomit? I didn't know how, and besides, the pills were already beginning to affect me. The room was tilting back and forth and my head felt like it was expanding. I panicked. Shannon and Joey were at home with me. I hadn't even thought about them. What was going to happen to them? I didn't know what to do. I couldn't put this in Katie's lap. She was just a kid for crying out loud. She was probably just 18 or 19 at the time. But I didn't know what to do. So I told her what I'd done.

"Hang up right now and call 9-1-1," she said. "I'm on my way."

I told Joey I was going outside and that he was to stay in the house with Shannon, no matter what.

And I went out onto my carport, laid down on the concrete and called 9-1-1.

Things got very blurry after that, but I know that the kids didn't stay inside. There was a fire truck in our driveway, after all. And an ambulance, and police cars. I could hear Shannon. I couldn't see her, and it sounded like she was very far away, but she was freaking out. "Help her," I kept saying. At least, I think I was saying it. "Help her." I could also hear Hooch. He was doing his best to break through the kitchen door and onto the carport. I know that, because the firemen were afraid of him. They kept talking to me, asking me questions. "What had I taken?" "Had I had anything to drink?" I answered them, but they kept asking me, over and over. I kept blanking out, but I knew Katie had arrived. I could see her, arms folded, standing outside the doors of the ambulance with our next-door neighbor. She was a very nice lady. I don't remember her name, but she saw me at my utter worst. She saw me at the worst any person can be.

And then I remember waking up in the hospital. I don't know how long I was out, but there was a nurse there. She leaned over me and said, "Your daughter is something else! She won't leave, and she's insisting that we let her come back to see you. Is that okay?"

So all three children came back to sit with their crazy mother in the hospital room after she tried to leave them behind.

Then the doctor came and made them leave. They were going to pump my stomach.

Whenever Aries would colic, we would call the vet out and he would pump mineral oil into Aries' stomach. They would run a tube up his nostril and down his throat, into his stomach. Aries hated it with a passion, and I always felt so bad for him, but I wanted him to get better.

They did exactly the same thing to me. It was a disgusting, excruciatingly painful experience. They shoved a huge tube up my nose. I think it was the same size the vet used for Aries. And it stopped. Something was in the way. So they got three nurses to push on the damn thing until it broke through whatever body part was blocking its path. I was strapped down to the bed, so I couldn't do anything about it but grit my teeth and try not to scream. I wasn't sure how far away the kids were, and I didn't want them to hear me scream.

I have no idea how long we were there, but eventually, they moved me somewhere else.

For the first time in my life, I was supposed to have health insurance, through my brand-new job at FC&A, but there had been a mix-up and my insurance had not been processed yet. I wasn't covered.

And people who attempt suicide without insurance coverage go to the state mental hospital. In the back of a police car. In handcuffs. Apparently, it's illegal to kill yourself. But who knew?

It was a long drive in the middle of the night. I could see the burly policeman looking at me in the rearview mirror. He looked angry. He looked like he hated me. I didn't mind, because he couldn't hate me as much as I hated me.

And then he spoke. "I know this is none of my business," he said. "But I've been a policeman for 21 years, and I've driven a lot of people down this road. Mostly women. Mostly over some man, who never even shows up at the hospital. Sometimes, someone will show up. A friend or a parent. For most people, no one comes. But never, not once in 21 years, have I *ever* seen an entire family insist on following me to the hospital."

In that dark night, on the freeway behind us, was a little red Ranger pickup truck with three of the greatest kids anyone has ever been blessed with.

I couldn't answer him. I couldn't defend myself. There was no defense. So he went on.

"Ma'am, you've got something back there. You need to straighten yourself out and take care of those kids."

I think I managed to whimper a "yes sir." I could not believe I had sunk so low. Me. The one who always, always put my kids first. I had done the most selfish thing anyone could do. I was scum.

When we got to the hospital, they took my handcuffs off and then asked me some questions. Name, date of birth, etc. And then the nurse asked me if I knew who the current president was. I did. "Bill Clinton," I answered.

"And before him?"

"Ronald Reagan."

"And before him?"

This was a test, and I was good at tests. If I could make myself focus, even though my head was still a little airy-feeling, and answered all the questions right, maybe they would let me out of this awful place.

"Jimmy Carter."

The nurse ran down the list of presidents, going faster and faster. I concentrated really hard, and I didn't miss a single one. I know I didn't.

Then he got up and said, "Okay, we're going to take your picture now, and then we'll get you settled in for the night."

"But I got all the answers right," I thought.

They took me to a little room, where Katie was waiting for me.

"We tried to make her leave," the nurse said. "She says she won't until she makes sure you're okay."

So Katie sat with me while we filled out paperwork. She wouldn't let me sign anything until she read it. When the nurse said something about prosecution, Katie got downright angry. "Does she need a lawyer?" she demanded. "No one has told us she needs a lawyer, but if she needs one, I'll get one!"

The nurse assured her that I didn't need a lawyer, and convinced her that I would be okay. By then, my senses were beginning to come back, and I managed to pull myself together enough to invoke a tiny bit of my motherly authority and convinced her to go and take Shannon and Joey home.

The state mental hospital is a very scary place. It is just filled to the gills with crazy people. People who make strange noises in the middle of the night. All night long.

They took my shoes and gave me neon-orange foam slippers. I was supposed to sleep on a cot, in a big room with just partitions between me and all the other crazy people. And although I had only recently taken a large number of sleeping pills, I didn't sleep a wink in that place.

The next morning, when I heard people begin stirring about, I got up and asked where the bathroom was. I went in and washed my face off. I looked into the mirror above the sink. I was shocked by what I saw. My eyes were still dilated. I looked wild and disheveled. I looked like I belonged in the state mental hospital. I tried to comb my hair out with my fingers, and then I went back out into the big room.

The nurse at the desk told me to go wash my face.

"Oh, I just washed my face," I replied, and kept walking.

Suddenly, she was standing in front of me, hands on her hips. "You can go wash your face," she said, "Or I can get some orderlies to come drag you in there and make you wash it."

I almost laughed. Was she joking? Did she think she was Nurse Ratched or something? But she was dead serious, and since I'd recently been strapped to a bed and had a tube shoved up my nose, I knew they could do it. And judging by her attitude, she'd probably enjoy doing it.

So I went and washed my face again. And she told me to eat breakfast. I said I wasn't hungry. And she told me I could eat my breakfast voluntarily or ... so I ate breakfast, or at least pretended to.

The nurse from the night before, the nice one, had told me that I would get to see a psychiatrist in the morning, and that if he cleared me, I could go home. And this nightmare would be over, and I could start working on making things right again.

So I waited for my turn and finally got to see the doctor. I was still wearing the same clothes I'd worn the day before, and I had neon-orange foam slippers on, and I knew my eyes were wild-looking and my hair was a mess. But I sat in the chair across from the psychiatrist, crossed my legs, folded my hands in my lap, sat up straight, and tried to look sane and civilized.

He wanted me to say I did it to punish people. I tried to tell him that wasn't the reason. That I wasn't thinking, "Oh, they'll be sorry when they don't have me to kick around any more." If I had gotten that far in the thought process, I never would have done it. He told me I was angry. I said, no, I wasn't. I was tired. He said, no, I was angry. I was angry because I'd been mistreated, and I wanted to make people hurt the way they had hurt me.

But if I had known, if I had been thinking clearly, if I had realized how hurt my children would be, there's no way I would have done what I did. I wasn't out to hurt *anyone*. Not Sam, not my kids. That wasn't it. I was exhausted. I'd been struggling for so long, trying to hold it together, I just had a momentary ... disruption of brain function.

But he wanted me to say I was angry. That I was being vindictive. So I said it. I just wanted to get out of there, and I knew he wasn't really interested in why I did it. He knew nothing about me, any more than he knew anything about the dozens of other people he would see that day. He wasn't there to help me, or anyone else. He was there to collect a paycheck.

So he signed my release form and I was free to go. Free to start trying to make amends for the damage I'd done to my children.

I called Katie, and asked her to come pick me up. She told me she'd be there as soon as she got off work. And so I had to cool my heels in that awful place for a few more hours. It was the longest hours I'd ever endured. And it was the least I deserved.

When she finally arrived, I got in the truck and shut the door. I didn't know what to say. "I'm sorry" didn't seem adequate. So I didn't say anything.

"You ok?" she asked.

I nodded.

"You need something to eat?"

I shook my head.

"You want to go home?"

I shook my head again.

"Where do you want to go?"

And I still couldn't answer. All I could do was sit there with my head hanging and cry.

But she didn't need me to answer. She knew where I needed to go. And so she pulled out of the parking lot of the mental hospital and headed toward Rock House Ranch. Away from crazy. Toward sanity. Toward Aries.

19 MIDDLE OF NOWHERE

I was determined to make things right with my kids and move on with my life. And to never, ever, let the crazy out again.

But when out of nowhere, Sam wanted to get back together, I couldn't resist. I couldn't help it. I loved him and I was ecstatic that he was back. I finally met his family and we started to talk about getting married.

But relationships hinge on trust, and the trust was gone. For both of us. We tried, but things would never be the same between us. I knew it, he knew it, and even Hooch knew it.

One night Sam and I were in the kitchen, making dinner. As we moved back and forth between refrigerator, stove, table and sink, we were arguing. Nothing major, just disagreeing about something. But as we stopped near the kitchen counter, we both became aware that the entire time we'd been in the kitchen, Hooch had been positioning himself very subtly between us. But since we were now a mere couple of feet apart, his presence was no longer subtle. His haunches were resting on my shoes, and his front paws were near Sam's feet, his head upraised, fixed on Sam's face.

Sam and I looked down and then at each other with the silent realization of Hooch's protective instincts. And Sam said, "I wonder what he'd do if I..." and as he said the word "I," he leaned forward, grabbing me by the shoulders with both hands.

It happened so fast, I didn't have time to react. Didn't have time to say, "Don't be stupid, Sam." Didn't have time to say, "There, Hooch. It's ok." In an instant, I just knew that Sam's hands were gripping my shoulders. And knew that Hooch was between us.

He never growled. Never made a sound. But his front paws were now on Sam's chest, and he was looking him in the eye, his nose practically touching Sam's. I held my breath, because I knew how ugly and bloody this situation could turn out to be. I didn't dare move my head, but shifted my eyes downward. And I could see that Hooch's lips were drawn back from his teeth in a quiet but unmistakable message. "Back off. Or else."

And Sam very carefully let go of my shoulders and took a step backwards. Hooch dropped to the floor, but his eyes were still trained on Sam's face. In fact, from that moment on, whenever he was in the house, Hooch's eyes were always fixed on Sam.

I can't say that the final break occurred because of Hooch's distrust of Sam. But I have to admit that I took it into consideration. As much as I loved Sam, it was time to let him go.

And as usual, I turned to Aries for comfort. We went on long trail rides, just the two of us, and he listened to my silly prattle with little more than a few backward flicks of his ear. He was always patient, always grateful for his apples ... he was, as always, my rock.

But as comforting as Aries' presence was, we are a species that is compelled to seek out the company of our own kind. And so I tried dating again. Since my weight loss, I was relatively attractive, and men to date weren't hard to find. Men who would stick around, once they found out about my circumstances, were much more difficult to find. And finding a man who would stick around that I could also love proved impossible.

Once, when I was lamenting my permanently single status to my brother, he told me, "Men are all about responsibility, Tammy. And you come with more responsibility than most women." It was a line almost straight from Spiderman. He'd always been a comic book fan.

He was talking about Shannon, of course. I already knew it. I'd already had the discussions, seen the subtle change of expressions, the abrupt disconnect of possibility. Many men didn't want to date women with kids at all, much less a woman with a kid who would never grow up and leave home.

One of my final dates proved to be the last straw. I was doing the online dating thing, which was still in its infancy, but growing in popularity. It was a scary proposition at times, and I'd had a couple of bad encounters and had learned to be cautious. I tried not to tell anyone where I lived, or any especially revealing information, until I met them in person, at a public place.

We met at a popular restaurant near the Atlanta airport. He was interesting and attractive and it all seemed to be going well. I told him about Katie, who trained horses for a living, and Joey, who was in high school at the time and already seven feet tall and playing basketball. Men were always fascinated to hear about Joey.

Then he said, "But you have three kids, right? What about the other one?"

I felt myself tense up. I'd had this conversation dozens of times, and I'd developed a chip on my shoulder the size of Stone Mountain. The reactions I'd gotten were varying degrees of negative. And I would find myself gushing on about how wonderful Shannon was. Which she was. She was amazingly funny and kind and generous and smart. She could have blown them away with her sports knowledge. She was like a walking encyclopedia of Braves history. And then I would feel like I was trying to "sell" her to them, which would make me a little angry. Angry at them and at me.

So I told him a little bit about Shannon, and watched that facial expression change that I'd become so familiar with. That little withdrawal. But this guy, for whatever reason, decided to plunge ahead and try to "fix" the situation.

"So ... she lives with you?" he asked, clearly disapproving of this development.

"Yes." I replied. "And she always will," I added for complete disclosure and clarification.

"Well, don't you think maybe you're being a little selfish?"

This was a new one. I was confused and offended. "Ummm, no. Why?"

"Don't you think she'd be happier in one of those group homes?"

Now I understood his angle, and I gritted my teeth and tried to keep a semblance of a pleasant expression on my face. "No, I don't."

And then he uttered a sentence that was so full of idiotic, just *wrong* phrases that it is emblazoned into my memory banks, verbatim, forever.

He said, "Well, *I've heard* that *those people* are happier when they're *with their own kind.*"

About the time this exchange took place, our food arrived. I was looking down at my plate. I'd ordered steak. I never ordered steak. And it looked good. Hot and steaming. With a shiny, sharp steak knife lying across the edge of the plate.

I looked at that plate and I thought, "If I stay here, one of two things are going to happen. I'm going to start crying, which would be bad. Or, I'm going to pick up that steak knife and stab this guy in the throat, which would be worse."

So instead, I looked up from the plate, away from the steak knife. I looked him in the eye and said, "This date is over."

And I got up and walked out.

Eventually, I decided that the thought I'd had that day ... the thought that, if I couldn't make it work with Sam, I couldn't make it work with anyone .. was true. But it was okay.

We as a species may be genetically driven to pair up, but not everyone is destined to be Cinderella. And I was way more comfortable in a pair of paddock boots than glass slippers, anyway.

* * *

Katie had grown up and left home, having taken a job as manager at a hunter/jumper farm in Atlanta. The job came with a house, so she lived on the farm. It was tough for me, my first child leaving home, but she was nearby, so I still saw her fairly often.

Her job change meant that Aries no longer had free board at Rock House, so we had to say goodbye to the old red barn, to the arena where

I'd had my first horse show, to the pasture where I'd walked myself back to health and happiness.

Eventually, one of Katie's friends stepped forward to offer us a new home for Aries.

Michelle and Brian lived in a small house on five acres at the end of a dirt road, only a few miles from Rock House. They had a little two-stall barn where Michelle's Arabian mare, Sierra, lived. Sierra and Aries were old friends, as she used to board at Rock House as well. Katie and Michelle had been to numerous horse shows together. I still have a photo of Katie jumping Sierra, bridleless, after they had won a championship in an A-rated Arabian show.

It was the perfect arrangement for me. It was still close to home, and I was welcome to come see Aries any time I wanted. And Brian and Michelle were wonderful, salt-of-the-earth type people who I enjoyed seeing. My life may have taken some unwanted turns, but I still had my kids, my job, and of course, Aries.

And then one day, I was going to visit Aries and was shocked to see a "For Sale" sign at the end of Brian and Michelle's driveway. My anxiety immediately kicked into overdrive and I began to fret about Aries. If they sold this place, wherever would we go? Whatever would we do?

When I expressed my dismay to them, Brian said, "Well, you could just buy it for yourself."

Me? Buy a house? Of my own? The thought was overwhelming and exciting. My husband and I had never owned a house, going from living with his parents to a dingy rental trailer to another dingy rental trailer and another. I was still living in the rental house that my brother had once kicked me out of. Owning a home was a segment in my frequent fantasies of the future, but the reality, while exciting, was also a little bit terrifying. I had no clue how to even start, I didn't have a credit history, and I didn't have any money saved for a down payment.

I discussed it with my coworkers at FC&A and discovered that one of the many unique benefits they offered their employees was down payment assistance for first-time home buyers. They would actually give me money for a down payment! I was stunned.

Another coworker at FC&A had recently left to pursue a career as a real estate agent, so I gave her a call. She put me in touch with a mortgage broker. I was worried because my credit history was spotty at best. But it was the era of creative financing and soon I was the extremely proud owner of five acres with a house, a garage, a barn and a pasture for Aries. And an adjustable rate mortgage. Cue ominous music.

My inexperience meant that my price negotiations for the property went about as well as my interview for FC&A. Brian called me and asked if my agent and I were going to send them an offer. Since this was long before I got hooked on *Property Brothers*, and I'd never bought or sold a house before, I didn't have a clue. They were asking $104,000 and my agent had said that was a good price for five acres. So that's what I told Brian.

There was a long pause on the other end of the line, and then I heard a heavy sigh. "We'll take 102 and we'll pay half the closing costs," he said.

It was probably the first time in the history of real estate that the *seller* negotiated the price down.

My co-workers were nearly as excited as I was about my new house, and I planned a housewarming party shortly after I moved so I could show it off to them. I also wanted to show Aries off, as they heard me talk about him all the time. I thought that perhaps they weren't totally convinced that he was the most beautiful horse in the world, and that they should see him in the flesh, for proof.

I had added a couple of dogs to my menagerie in the years since that walk in the dark with Twinkie, Muffin, and Hooch. Muffin had passed away, and I had inherited a dog from Sam. Pixel was a Lab/Dalmatian cross. She was white, with solid black ears and she had spots like a Dalmatian, but her spots were smaller. The name Pixel suited her perfectly, and reflected Sam's interest in computers. She didn't do well in his apartment, however, and so she came to live with me. After Sam and I broke up, she just stayed with us. Pixel probably loved me more than any dog I've ever had. You could just see it in her eyes when she looked at me. Everyone should have a dog (or better yet, a person) who looks at them the way Pixel looked at me.

And we had also added a dog named Trouble to our pack. Trouble was a Catahoula, and the most incredibly athletic dog I'd ever seen. She was also certifiably crazy. Trouble provided me with a vast supply of stories to tell, and one of them occurred at my housewarming party.

Angela, my manager at FC&A, had asked if she could bring her dogs to the party. I had plenty of room for them to run around, and my dogs were pretty sociable with other dogs, so of course I told her yes. She owned a Sheltie and a Rhodesian Ridgeback.

The day of the party arrived and I was standing on my deck, talking to the early arrivals, when Angela's truck pulled down my driveway. She drove a Ford Ranger, like mine, which had an area behind the front seats with folding seats that you could either fold down for passengers, or stow up, for more storage space. Angela had folded her seats up, and had her dogs in that storage space. The Sheltie was fairly small, but the Ridgeback took up most of the space. The truck also had a sliding window that opened up into the bed of the pickup. Angela had that window open, so her dogs could get air.

We watched Angela's truck pulling up the driveway, when suddenly it screeched to a halt, and Angela jumped out, flinging her door open and turning to fold her seat forward. When she did, dogs just exploded out of the truck like clowns out of a Volkswagen at the circus. Chaos ensued for a few minutes, as Angela's daughter joined in, trying to help separate the seething mass of dogflesh that seemed to just keep coming out of the truck. I could see Trouble's mottled brown coat circling with the Ridgeback's tawny muscular body, and the Sheltie just seemed to be trying to get out of everyone's way. Fortunately, none of the dogs involved were being aggressive and Angela soon had everything under control.

That's when I learned that, as Angela was driving down my driveway, Trouble had jumped into the bed of her *moving* pickup and then into the small sliding glass window that led into the truck. Which landed her smack dab between Angela's two dogs, who were startled – probably completely freaked out – by the sudden appearance of a strange dog in the already cramped space they were sharing.

The remainder of the party proceeded without a hitch and Aries gave short rides around the yard to anyone who wanted one. I was surprised that that wasn't every single person. I had always been so enamored of horses, it was hard to imagine anyone turning down an opportunity for a free ride.

I now had the opportunity to ride pretty much whenever I wanted. Behind and beside my property was a thousand-acre timber farm. They had only recently cut the timber off of it, and so at the time, it was scarred and ugly, with broken tree carcasses littering the landscape. The property was leased by a hunting club, and they had trails that wound around and through the property – a large track where they drove their trucks, and smaller ones where they would take their four-wheelers. It was perfect for riding. It did occur to me that I didn't have permission from anyone to ride back there, but unless someone told me not to do it, I was going to take advantage of it. I just avoided it mostly during deer season, sticking to riding up and down my dirt road, or just around my yard and pasture instead.

But what brought me the most joy was just Aries' proximity. I could see his pasture from my kitchen window, or I could sit on the deck and watch him grazing. My coworkers had all chipped in and bought me a mailbox for my new house. Camilla, who was very artistically inclined, painted a picture of Aries' beautiful head on one side, and the words "Middle of Nowhere Farm" on the other side. Aries and I were officially home.

20 Sparky

I stood in the driveway of my still-new home and tried to fight back the tears. Katie hated it when I cried.

She had her whole life packed into her truck. She had taken a job at a horse farm in Virginia and she was leaving to go where she didn't know a single soul. The trainer she was going to be working for was well known and respected ... a World Cup level show jumper. And the job was a great opportunity for her, a change of pace and scenery in an area of some of the most elite horse farms in the world. But Virginia was a long way from Georgia, and I was worried. I was worried about her and about me. She was going to be truly alone there, and I had always leaned on her so much, that I felt as if I was going to be alone as well.

One last flurry of motherly warnings and advice, and she got into her truck, Hooch riding shotgun, and drove away down my driveway. As I watched her truck go, with not much in it but her clothes, her saddle, her guitar and her dog, I realized that beneath my worry and fear was another emotion – a familiar one, and yet one I was surprised to recognize in this particular situation.

I was jealous. She was embarking on a great adventure, one that in-volved a beautiful farm with top-notch horses and a world of possibilities. I realized how much I would have loved to have been in her shoes when I was her age. The odd sensation of jealousy was quickly replaced with pride. She was fearless and tough, and she had Hooch to protect her. She was going to be fine. She was going to be brilliant.

I turned and saw Aries watching me from the fence. He had helped send Katie on this path. He was her first real hunter/jumper and he had taken her from 4-H shows and schooling shows to A-rated shows, and had been a vehicle for her students (including her mother) to learn and grow and earn ribbons of their own, while Katie grew in her role as a trainer and instructor.

I went inside to get him an apple. He deserved it.

* * *

Shortly after I moved into the house, I was presented with a new problem. Michelle took Sierra to her new place, which left Aries alone. Horses are herd animals and appreciate the company of others, so I needed to find him a buddy.

I could buy another horse, but instead I decided to check out one of the horse rescue groups in the area to find an older, companion horse for Aries. I still remembered the kindness of the people who took Pibb on as a companion horse, caring for him even though he was virtually unrideable. I wanted to take this opportunity and pay it forward.

I saw an ad online and called the number. It was a polo farm in North Georgia somewhere, and the man I spoke to told me that the horse in question had already found another home. But he said he had another horse that also needed someone to take him. It was a retired polo pony that was just living in his pasture and the owner didn't really have time for him. He was 26 years old and needed a home with a little TLC. I liked to think that I'd always been pretty good at TLC, so I made an appointment to go look at the horse.

I drove up on a pretty fall Saturday, and parked in front of a very nice barn. Lots of people were out, and they were dressed in oddly nice clothing for a barn on a Saturday. I was used to seeing dusty boots and grubby jeans at barns on weekends, but here there were women strolling around in sundresses and floppy hats, sipping mimosas from plastic champagne glasses. At least I assumed they were plastic. Maybe they were real crystal. Nobody offered me one, so I didn't have an opportunity to find out.

There was apparently some sort of event going on. I saw several striped canopies set up near the polo fields, which were located down a hill and to the right of the barns. There seemed to be quite a spread set out under those canopies, with snacks and beverages. And there were people playing polo. I'd never seen a polo match in person, so I stood and watched, enthralled by the spectacle and fantasizing about being Julia Roberts at a polo match in a sundress and floppy hat.

After a few moments, I decided it was time to see a woman about a horse, so I turned to look around the barn area. And that's when I saw him, standing spraddle-legged, his head hanging down. He was skinny and his coat was dull and rough. I watched as a sleek, shiny polo pony jogged past him, all braided and groomed, and was struck by the contrast. As I approached the woman holding him, he didn't even lift his head. He didn't seem to notice me at all.

I didn't even introduce myself. "I'll take him," were the first words out of my mouth.

And so Sparky, the retired polo pony, came to live with Aries and me in the middle of nowhere.

It is a regrettable fact that bad things sometimes happen to horses that outlive their usefulness. Being left alone in a pasture was not the worst case scenario. Horses are expensive to take care of properly. Feed bills, vet bills, farrier bills, medications, dewormers … it all adds up. Throw in the labor to feed, hay, water, and sometimes medicate an aging horse, and you can see why some people aren't willing to put all that time, effort and money into a horse that can't speed around a polo field or clear 4-foot fences anymore.

I believe that Sparky, at one time, was a magnificent polo pony. I bet he was fearless and fast. I am sure that as he got a little older, he took care of numerous aspiring young polo players, teaching them the ropes with care and grace. I'm sure that at one time, he was a pampered pony, enjoying a warm, dry stall, lots of hay and grain, and plenty of carrots and apples. So while being stuck out in a pasture may not have been the worst thing that could have happened to him, I'm sure it wasn't what he was used to.

I'm sure my little place wasn't what he was used to, either, but I think he liked it. He and Aries got along well. By now, Aries was in his late teens himself, and was pretty mellow. I had two stalls, and the doors opened up into the pasture, so I just left the doors open, so they could come and go as they pleased.

Aries had already staked out one of the stalls as his, so Sparky naturally took the other one. I think he loved his stall. And I think he really loved his blanket. I'm not sure why I thought that, but I believe it. There was just something about the way he held himself as I would settle the blanket onto his back. He would stand very still, but he would lift his head and expand his chest, as if the blanket somehow made him more important. I felt so strongly about my blanket theory, that I ordered him a new, heavier one for the winter. Besides, he was so thin, I was sure he felt the cold acutely.

I started out feeding Sparky small amounts of feed, gradually increasing it until he was eating pretty much the same as Aries. He started to fill out and his coat grew shinier with frequent grooming. He began to hold his head up and actually look at me.

Everything was ideal until I added a third horse to the mix. My brother had to leave town unexpectedly, leaving his horse Deb in the pasture of the house he was renting. So I brought Deb to my house.

Deb was a grey Arabian gelding whose registered name was Ramses Debonair. He came from the same herd at Talaria that Khan did. They didn't share any direct breeding, but they were both straight Egyptian. The Ramses horses were named in alphabetical sequence, with the obvious Ramses prefix. Khan was born in 1985, which was an "A" year, so his name was Ramses Ali Khan. Deb was born in a "D" year, so his name was Ramses Debonair. It was a handy way to keep track of how old each horse was. And Deb was a good bit younger than Aries and much younger than Sparky.

Deb had also been alone in the pasture at my brother's house, and wasn't used to sharing. Horses, like most herd animals, have a pecking order. Some horses are dominant and bossy. Others are content to stand back and let others take the lead. Deb had a strong drive for dominance. It didn't matter much to Aries, as he was a good bit bigger than Deb, relatively dominant and not that much older than Deb.

Sparky was another story, as Deb asserted himself to the weakest horse in the three-horse pasture. He would charge at Sparky ferociously, ears pinned and teeth bared. Feeding time became a struggle. I was used to just putting Aries and Sparky's feed in their stalls and being done with it. I tried to continue feeding them in their stalls and feeding Deb in a feed pan outside the stalls, but if I left the doors open, as I'd been doing, Deb would run into Sparky's stall and chase him out. Then, if he saw that Sparky was eating *his* food, he'd try to run him away from that as well. So I had to shut them in the stalls until everyone was finished eating.

The ideal situation of being able to leave the stall doors open was also no longer ideal, because whenever Sparky tried to go in his stall, Deb would go in and run him out. I needed to build another stall, but that was going to take some time. I hated to shut the doors, because if it started to rain while I was gone, they wouldn't have any shelter.

Deb had been with us only about a week, when I came home to find Sparky down on his side in the pasture. He was in obvious distress, and there was blood coming out of his mouth and nostrils. I ran inside to call a vet. Johnny Pritchard, our beloved JP, had had some health problems and was semi-retired, so I had been unable to get in touch with him since leaving Rock House. So I just had to pick a name out of the Yellow Pages.

I don't remember the vet's name now, and it didn't matter, because by the time he got there, Sparky was gone. I was right beside him, talking to him at the end. I hope that brought him some comfort. He'd been with me just less than a year, and I hope that I did the right thing by bringing him to the middle of nowhere. I, of course, felt guilty, wondering if he'd have been better off if I'd left him where he was. But I knew that in the months that I'd had him, his body had grown stronger, his eyes had grown brighter, and he seemed happy. Much happier than the skinny, head-hanging horse I'd first seen. So although I beat myself up over every decision I ever make, I think that the decision to bring Sparky home with me was the right one, despite the heart-wrenching end.

And then I was faced with another upsetting, but practical problem … what to do with his body. I went inside and made some calls and found a backhoe operator who was willing to come bury him. I shut the blinds and stayed inside the house, unwilling to view him lying in the pasture. When the guy knocked on my door, he asked me if I wanted him to take the blanket off Sparky. I told him no.

"Are you sure?" he asked, "It looks like a nice one."

"No," I snapped. "That blanket is his."

21 DEBONAIR

ARIES and Deb co-existed peacefully in the pasture. I didn't get the sense that they were exactly bosom buddies, but perhaps I was projecting my feelings toward Deb onto Aries. I think I was still a little resentful of Deb, because of the way he'd acted toward Sparky.

Deb was exhibiting perfectly normal equine behavior, of course. It's their instinct to establish themselves and their position in the herd. My human instinct, though, was to regret the fact that Sparky's last days weren't as peaceful as the rest of his time here had been. And while I primarily blamed myself (I should have separated them, I should have done this, I should have done that), I think I still placed some blame on Deb, and it colored my perception of him. Also, Deb hadn't been handled that much in his life, and wasn't as human-friendly as a lot of horses.

Aries and I would go on long trail rides on the property behind my house. At first, because the trail was littered with fallen trees, I would saddle up and we would ride for hours, often jumping over small logs. I never failed to get a thrill from jumping, even though it was barely a hop over. The sensation of flying as his hooves left the ground was one that I could completely understand people getting hooked on. I can still watch Olympic show jumping on television, and get that same little feeling in the pit of my stomach as I watch those amazing creatures and riders soar over huge fences.

Over the years, the property that was once scarred and ugly would grow and turn lush and green with new trees and bushes, while Aries and I would grow older and slower. Our rides would become shorter and less frequent. We would no longer jump over anything, and I would no longer bother putting a saddle on him. Eventually, I wouldn't even put a bridle on him, preferring instead to simply hop up on him bareback with a halter and lead rope.

One reason I thought that Deb and Aries weren't that attached was because, when Aries and I would go off for a ride, Deb didn't seem to mind. Many pasture mates get upset whenever they are separated, but Aries and Deb seemed to not even notice if the other one wasn't there.

And then something happened that changed the whole dynamic between the three of us. Deb scratched his cornea.

I still hadn't found a regular vet that I trusted in the same way I had trusted JP. There was one woman I really liked, but her practice was so far away that she was an impractical choice in an emergency. It would take her too long to reach us. I needed to find a good vet who was close to home.

I found that there was a new vet practicing in the area, so I decided to call her. She gave me two medicines that had to be put in Deb's eye four times a day. Imagine, if you will (those of you who haven't tried it), making a 1,000 pound animal stand still while you put drops AND cream into his eye. Deb didn't trust me the way Aries did, and he was not cooperative. At first, I would have Shannon try to hold onto his lead rope, so I could have both hands free to get the medicine into his eye, but once he tossed his head and smacked her in the face pretty hard, she was done. I was on my own.

It was a frustrating process, and yet I knew that I had to get the medicine in if his eye was going to heal. I would stand with the lead rope clinched between my knees, loop one arm up and around his neck and use it to try to hold his eyelid open, while I applied the medicine with the other hand.

Deb could probably have simply bolted away. He was certainly strong enough. But he didn't. He just jigged around and tossed his head and squirmed like a three year old getting his first haircut. My arms would grow tired and my patience would grow thin. And then one day, during this struggling sort of dance we were doing, Deb suddenly became completely still. I was surprised and elated. He must have finally realized that what I was doing was for his own good. He must have had a sudden epiphany. He had realized that I wasn't the bad guy. I was trying to help him. I was able to get the medicine in more easily than I ever had, and I released him, feeling exceedingly pleased with myself.

And that's when I saw Aries. He was standing on the other side of Deb, and he had a fold of skin from Deb's neck pinched between his teeth. I was stunned. He had been watching us, and had decided to try to help. He effectively was twitching Deb for me.

For non-horse people, a twitch is a device horse owners sometimes use to keep a horse still while you're trying to work on them. Some are made of metal and others consist of a long wooden handle with a rope loop on the end of it. The process is to pinch the horse's upper lip into the rope loop and then tighten it down until the horse stands still.

Some people think this is cruel. I've heard others say that it doesn't hurt and that it simply has a strange calming effect on the horse. Personally, I think it probably hurts like hell. But sometimes it's the only way to get them to stand still and it's for their own good.

What Aries was doing, pinching Deb's skin like that, had worked in the same way. Amazingly, it became a routine, and every time I had to medicate Deb, Aries would "hold" him for me.

Unfortunately for all of us, especially for Deb, it didn't do much good. Because I walked out to the pasture one day to put the medicine in and I discovered that Deb's eyeball had ruptured. I cannot adequately describe the horror I felt when I saw it. It was one of the most grotesque and disturbing things I have ever seen. And I can't imagine the kind of pain he must have been in. I also cannot describe how angry I was with the callous response of the vet when I called her. She seemed so nonchalant. Oh, yes, that happened sometimes. No, she couldn't come right now. No, she wouldn't let me come to her to get painkiller to make him comfortable until she *could* come. And I couldn't believe that she hadn't even explained to me that this was a possibility. A little heads up would have been nice. A quick, "Oh and by the way, sometimes the eyeball explodes." Her treatment was callous and I was furious.

I frantically made phone calls and rounded up a trailer that I could borrow. I also borrowed some painkiller from a friend, and made Deb as comfortable as I could. Then we drove to Auburn University.

The large animal clinic at Auburn is about an hour and a half from my house. I had already taken Aries there once, during a prolonged bout with colic. The vets and students are always the epitome of professionalism and kindness, and the facilities are top notch.

I wish I had taken Deb there sooner. Maybe they wouldn't have been able to save his eye, but they probably could have given us a more thorough and accurate prognosis from the beginning. But by the time we got there, all they could do was remove the eye. He spent a couple of days there and then came back home with his eyelid stitched shut.

The silver lining to the whole episode was that Deb was suddenly a changed horse. He and Aries seemed closer in the emotional sense, and definitely were closer in the physical sense. Deb tended to not stray more than a few feet from Aries' side. I suppose that he followed Aries around because of his newly limited field of vision. But he also seemed more affectionate toward me. When I went into the pasture, he would automatically come my direction. Maybe it was because Aries did and he was just following suit, but he also became much sweeter and easier to work with. For example, instead of snatching apples and carrots from my hand and dashing off, he would take them more gently and stand near me to eat them. Aries, spoiled thing that he was, would eat his apple bite by tiny bite from my hand as I stood there holding it. It didn't matter how long it took. He knew I'd hold it for him. So while Deb didn't give me the same level of trust and love that Aries did, he had certainly come around to thinking that I was pretty ok. And I was pretty ok with that.

22 Communicator

Hooch was coming home. Katie was traveling a lot to different horse shows, and Hooch was getting older, so it was hard on both of them. As excited as I was to have him back home, I (of course) worried about Katie being alone. I had counted on Hooch to keep an eye on her for me. And even though Katie had gotten Hooch as a present for me, his heart belonged to her and it always would.

As much as he missed Katie, I think Hooch enjoyed being back with the other dogs, even though Trouble's antics probably got on his nerves. I had a fenced in area behind my garage that Twinkie and Pixel stayed in, but there wasn't a fence built that could keep Trouble in, so she roamed the entire property as she pleased. Hooch was also free to roam, but he stayed close by, and unlike Trouble, always came when we called.

My birthday was coming up and Katie asked me what I wanted. She quickly added, "And don't say 'nothing'."

"But I really don't need anything," I protested.

"Well," said Katie, in a twist on a question I had asked her many years before, "What's something that you'd really like to have, but you would never buy for yourself?"

I knew the answer to that in a heartbeat. "I want to talk to Aries," I said.

The farm that Katie worked for sometimes used an animal communicator. If a horse had a health or training problem that they couldn't quite figure out, they would call her. And while the information might not be the most scientific, it did sometimes give them a different perspective to explore.

Katie had told me some stories about what other horses had "said" through this communicator, and while I wasn't 100 percent sold on the validity, I tend to be an open-minded person. I don't totally *disbelieve* much of anything. I just think it's a little arrogant to completely dismiss ideas, however outlandish. I mean, the idea that the world was round I'm sure seemed extremely outlandish to people at one point in time. And if a world-class caliber training facility used an animal communicator for horses that were worth hundreds of thousands of dollars, I shouldn't be embarrassed to use her.

I thought it would be entertaining at the least, and the idea of actually "talking" to Aries was too enticing to pass up. However, it wasn't something I would ever have spent money on myself. But as a gift … I was sold. Katie paid for it and made the arrangements. Strangely enough, it was done over the phone.

Today, animal communicators and "pet psychics" are becoming more and more popular and accepted. At least one famous pet psychic, Sonya Fitzpatrick, has had her own show on television. Some of these communicators say that they have a gift … that they are able to pick up energy and messages from animals, even over long distances. Most of them believe that animals are attempting to communicate with us telepathically all the time. We're just not all sensitive or open enough to receive it.

Most people, of course, say there is no scientific evidence that this kind of energy or communication exists. And I'm a big fan of science, but the funny thing about science is that it changes all the time. My favorite biology professor was fond of saying, "There's no such thing as proof." Scientists over the years have made discoveries that totally overturned the scientific "proof" that previously existed.

And so who was I to say that an animal communicator couldn't talk to Aries over the phone?

The communicator called at a prearranged time and we began to "talk" to Aries. She asked for his name and asked me to visualize him and to call to him with my mind, so that she could get a fix on him. We talked for a long time, but there were a few things she said that stood out.

She said, "He says you have two dogs."

I said, "I have four dogs."

Slight pause. "He says you have two dogs. He doesn't particularly like dogs. He thinks they're annoying and useless. Cats, he likes. Cats are useful. But he says that you have one dog ... a black dog. That one, he likes. He says that one is pretty laid back ... kind of a good old boy type of dog."

I had to admit that she nailed Hooch pretty well. He was definitely laid back.

Then she said, "But he says you have another dog. It's kind of a mottedly brownish-red type of color."

I had to smile at the way her tone changed when she said that. I could practically see her wrinkling her nose in distaste.

"Yeah, that's Trouble," I said.

"Yes, that's what he says," she responded.

"No, I mean her *name* is Trouble."

"Oh," she said. "Yeah, he doesn't like that one. He says that one has a sick sense of humor."

* * *

One night, Joey and I were trying to watch a movie in the living room. Trouble was outside, but kept scratching at the kitchen door. Caught up in the movie, we tried to ignore her, but finally Joey jumped up in exasperation and went to let her in. When he did, she ran through the kitchen, into the living room, jumped onto the couch and out of the living room window ... so she was back outside! I already had no screens in any of my windows, because Trouble would go right through them if she wanted out. Or in. That night, I had no idea why she couldn't have just gone around the house to get to the same point, but the term "sick sense of humor" made perfect sense.

* * *

I still wondered why the communicator would say I had two dogs instead of four, but later I was able to rationalize it because Twinkie and Pixel mostly stayed in the fenced in area behind my garage, which wasn't visible from Aries' pasture.

In fact, the longer she talked, the more I became convinced that the words were coming straight from Aries.

She said that he preferred being barefoot (which he now was since he was no longer showing and jumping) and that he had a farrier once who tried to "correct" his legs, but all it did was make him sore. Aries was a little pigeon-toed, and I did remember a farrier telling us he could shoe him so that it wouldn't be as noticeable. Just like she said, though, it only resulted in him limping around for a couple of weeks until we called the farrier back out to correct his corrective shoeing.

Then she said, "He's glad you're doing better, but he misses when you used to come see him in his stall in the middle of the night."

My heart lurched as I thought of those nights spent curled up on Aries' blanket on his stall floor during my short homeless period.

There was a bit of a lull in the conversation, while I relived that night and pondered my journey from desperate and homeless to living in my dream home with my best friend right in my backyard. Then she asked me if I believed in reincarnation.

It was an unexpected question, but as I've said, I don't totally disbelieve much of anything, and so that's what I told her.

"Because he says you've known each other before in a past life," she said. "In Scotland."

She probably also gave me a time period but I can't remember it, because I was a little surprised to hear Scotland mentioned. I'd always been fascinated by Scotland for some reason, (mostly men in kilts) but it wasn't a detail I really shared with anyone.

"In fact, he says you've known each other in several past lives, but you keep repeating the same pattern. Each time, he meets you too late. You're already married to another person ... a person who takes comfort from you but gives none in return. So in this life, he decided to come back as a horse, because you both loved horses. He thought that, as a horse, he might be able to break the cycle you always seem to repeat."

* * *

My marriage was definitely one that should never have happened. Seldom have there been two people more mis-matched and less meant for each other. But what does a sixteen-year-old know? Pretty much nothing. I was just a kid, and I thought I was in love. It wasn't until I actually fell in love that I understood the difference. Looking back, I realized that I wasn't in love and I didn't want a husband. I just wanted a protector. And I certainly wasn't what he needed or expected either.

He was obsessed with fitness and spent hours in the gym. I gained a ton of weight after Joey was born. I loved animals. He didn't. I wanted to stay home with the kids and avoid people. He wanted to go places and do things. He wanted to have fun.

And so he went out and had fun without me. Which I was actually somewhat ok with. Except when he threatened to leave me, at which point, I would panic. Because he was my protector. What would I do without my protector? We fell into a pattern of him leaving me or threatening to leave me every few months.

And I would cry and I would beg and I would promise to change. I'd lose weight. I'd keep the house cleaner. I'd learn to cook better. Whatever.

And so he'd stay. Or come back, after spending a few days somewhere else, most likely with someone else.

But then, Aries kicked him. And suddenly the pattern changed.

I wasn't there. He had taken Katie to the barn to turn the horses out and, although he never really had anything to do with the horses, he had decided to turn Aries out himself. He was in a hurry and thought he'd do it more quickly than Katie could.

Katie said that Aries didn't mean to do it. That he was just being exuberant and kicked out with one leg to the side. My husband didn't know that you should always hold the lead rope close to the horse's head, so you have more control, and you're in the safe zone. Instead, he was holding the end of the lead, as if he was walking a dog. That meant that there was enough space between them for Aries to clip him with a hoof when he kicked out.

He came home raging. We were getting rid of that horse, he said. In fact, we were getting rid of all of them. At the time, we had Ebony, Aries, and Pibb.

I protested that the girls loved the horses. That being at the barn was good for them. That selling the horses would break their hearts.

The horses were dangerous, he argued. They had broken my arm. What if they hurt one of the girls? Odd, I thought, that he hadn't demanded that we get rid of the horses after my broken arm. Or after Shannon had gotten kicked by another boarder's horse at Bar M.

And then he used the same tactic he had used successfully over and over for years. He threatened to leave.

"Either the horses go, or I go!" I could practically see the words hanging in the air between us, like grapes suspended in Jello. I felt a chill run up my spine, telling me that this was a pivotal moment. This was it, Tammy. Stand up. Have a backbone.

"You do whatever you think you have to do," I said. "But the horses aren't going anywhere."

And that was the end of my marriage. It would be a couple more years before it was physically over. Because he didn't leave that day. There would be more water under the bridge. More arguments. More differing points of views. But for me, that day was the end of my marriage.

So maybe I have to amend my previous statement that the horses didn't cause my divorce. They didn't. My marriage was one that should never have been. But the horses, and specifically Aries, did give me the courage to acknowledge that fact.

* * *

I considered the communicator's words. At this point, I had known Aries for more than twenty years. And in all that time, he had kicked exactly one person. So was it an accident? Or did he do it deliberately?

Still, I hung up the phone thinking that it was probably all just an act ... she probably said the exact same thing to dozens of other people. I wondered if she'd done research on me, but she lived in Virginia, and I lived in Georgia. This was before social media even existed as it does today, with people providing details of their everyday lives for anyone to look up online. And she only charged $50, so it wouldn't be worth her time to put very much effort into checking me out. All in all, it was a great birthday present and I was glad I did it, if for no reason other than it started a new habit.

Because I thought about what she said about Aries missing me coming to see him in the middle of the night.

Although I worked a 9-5 job at the time, all those years of working crazy hours long into the night had left me with a bad case of insomnia. Usually, when I would wake up at 3 a.m., I would just lie in bed, staring at the ceiling or I would try to watch television until I could go back to sleep. Or I would work on writing something if I had a freelance assignment. After talking to the communicator, however, I started keeping a flashlight and a bowl of apples beside my door. Whenever I would wake up in the middle of the night, I would grab that flashlight and an apple and go hang out with Aries for a while. It was a habit that would persist for years, and it was amazingly therapeutic.

It was also when I began to wonder in earnest how much Aries understood of our conversations. He was always eager to lend an ear in exchange for an apple or two. He was exceedingly fond of apples. But I began to notice that his response to me varied, depending on my mood. He had always had a very expressive face, and I began to read his expressions and the tone of his nickers more and more. Perhaps it was my imagination, perhaps the communicator had planted the seeds of anthropomorphization, but on those days when I was a little down and lonely, his greeting seemed more subdued and sympathetic – his nicker soft and deep. When I had exciting news or had a particularly good day, his greeting would be a little louder, a little more high-pitched. And then one night, I was horribly upset about something (I can't remember what now), and I leaned against his chest and put my arms around his neck. Aries' chest made a great sobbing spot. And after a moment, I felt a gentle pressure on my back. Aries had bent his head around and was squeezing me. He was giving me a hug.

23 BASKETBALL

WHEN we first moved to the Middle of Nowhere, Joey had just started high school. And now that I was working for FC&A, I suddenly had time to focus on him. No more notes on my pillow. No more pleading with me to stay with him.

Shannon was still at home, of course, having graduated high school with a special diploma. While she could never live on her own, she had become pretty self-sufficient. I continued to keep her involved in Special Olympics, and she spent her days hanging out with the dogs, helping take care of Aries and Deb, and following her beloved Braves. Despite what that doctor had told me all those years before, Shan was a perfectly adequate reader. She wasn't tempted to tackle *War and Peace*, but she could tell you who was on the 30-day disabled list for every major league baseball team, thanks to the wonder of the Internet.

Katie was gone, I had given up on having a social life, and there were no more horse shows to attend. Instead, basketball became the new center of my parental attention.

Joey had started playing basketball in middle school. When I attended his first game, I was shocked to find that the gym was completely packed. I had arrived a few minutes late, and could not find a seat. I had to watch the entire game standing up. I thought, "Wow, I never knew middle school basketball was so popular around here."

The following day, I picked up a newspaper at the gas station on my way to drop Joey off at school. He said there had been a reporter at the game, and there might be an article in the paper. He was right. The recap of the game said something like, "The gym was packed with a standing

room only crowd, most of them there to get a look at Whitewater's 6'8"
center, Joey Waldrop."

I was shocked again. All those people were there to see Joey? I was
so accustomed to his size, that I didn't realize how truly unusual it was.
A middle school basketball player who was already almost 7 foot tall
was intriguing to a lot of people. Joey was now the center of attention
almost everywhere he went. He played basketball with an AAU team,
and traveled all over for games and clinics.

Luckily for Joey, he hadn't inherited my social anxiety. In fact, he
thrived on the attention. In later years, he would grow tired of the "how's
the weather up there?" type of comments, but when he was in school,
I watched him patiently answer the same questions over and over, year
after year. "I'm 14 (or 15 or 16 or …)." "I'm 6'8" (or 6'9" or 6'10" or …).
"I wear a size 17 shoe (or 18 or 19 or 20)". We joked about getting him a
t-shirt made with all those answers on it, so he could just point to it and
skip all the questions. But the truth was, he enjoyed talking to most of
the people. Of course, there would come a time when all the attention
he got was not positive. There is an up side and a down side to almost
everything. Being that large often came in handy. He could change my
light bulbs without a step ladder, for instance. However, he also soon
learned that ceiling fans were his enemy.

Joey was so far from me on the introvert/extrovert scale in fact, that
drama became his passion. He loved performing. He was smart and
artistic, and pretty much the complete opposite of the big dumb jock
that people expected him to be. He landed a summer job as a street
performer at the Georgia Renaissance Festival. He was interviewed for
the position by a panel of seasoned Ren Fest performers. He told me it
went something like this:

Panelist 1: "How old are you?"

Joey: "15."

Panelist 2: "How tall are you?"

Joey: "Six foot, ten inches."

Panelist 3: "Wow, how'd you get so tall? How tall is your father?"

Joey: "About six foot two."

Panelist 2: "How tall is your mother?"

Joey: "Five-eight or so."

Panelist 1: "So essentially, you're just a freak."

Joey: "Yeah.... So I'd fit right in with you guys."

All the panelists laughed and agreed that he would fit right in with them. He worked at the Renaissance Festival all through high school and loved it. He loved it so much in fact, that he decided he wanted to get a degree in theatre when he went to college, which heavily affected his decision of which college he chose.

He chose the University of Georgia. Shannon was thrilled. She had been his biggest fan all through high school. When his team lost in the semi-finals of the state championship his senior year, Shannon cried. She was proud of him and fiercely protective of him, as he was of her.

Joey's freshman year, UGA's basketball team was extremely under-manned. The previous coach had left the cupboard bare, so to speak. There were only four seniors on the team and no juniors or sophomores. Still, the four seniors were all great players and they made a good season of it. One of the highlights was beating the University of Kentucky in the storied Rupp Arena in Lexington.

That game was thrilling, and one of my personal favorite memories. Joey didn't get much playing time, but he made his minutes count. As a basketball mom, seeing my son score points and block shots against a legendary team was exhilarating, even from the nose-bleed seats. However, he also managed to make enemies of a lot of die-hard Wildcat fans with one quote in the local newspaper. The reporter had approached him just moments after the victory, when the team was still jumping up and down in celebration of their win. The reporter asked him something vague about how it felt, and in the euphoria of victory, Joey responded with bravado. I can't remember the exact quote, but I know it did not come across well in the article. Joey was suddenly the target of hateful posts on the message boards and elsewhere on the Internet. Barbs which his sister saw and fretted over. They bothered me as well, but I especially didn't like Shannon reading them.

When the SEC tournament rolls around every year, Atlanta becomes known as "Catlanta," because of all the Kentucky Wildcat fans who come to watch. The entire town turns blue. Lexington, Kentucky is a town that backs their basketball team with a fervor, and they take over Atlanta with enthusiasm. Most of them are, of course, the epitome of decorum. However, we ran into a few who were not.

Shannon and I were beyond excited to be attending our first SEC tournament, and nervous as always to see Joey play. There was a separate line for family members and friends of the players to enter the games, as each player was allowed a certain number of free passes. The line was long, and Shannon and I were standing near a couple of girls in UGA t-shirts, and directly behind the mother of one of our cheerleaders. We chatted with the cheerleader's mother as we waited, when a group of inebriated Kentucky fans approached the girls behind us. They were drunken frat boys who had obviously been partying all night, and they had spotted the girls in their UGA apparel and began harassing them. The girls ignored them stonily, as the guys regaled them with tales of how badly their team was going to beat our team. They called our players various names, and I watched Shannon's face grow more and more distressed.

Then one of the guys said something like, "Your players are all going to be carted off the floor bloody." At the threat of physical violence toward our players, most especially her "little" brother, Shannon had had enough. She whipped around, thrusting her finger into the offending Cat fan's face, her shoulders squared and her face tense and angry. All she said was, "Hey, hey, now!" But the challenge was clear. She was throwing down in defense of her brother.

The bleary-eyed frat boy glared down at her, unsure of how to react to this strange challenge, but unwilling to back down in front of his friends. He puffed his chest out, as the mother of the cheerleader grabbed Shannon's hand and pulled her away, and allowed me to insert myself between them. I glanced around, looking for a security guard to call over to diffuse the situation, when I saw a wall of maroon to my left. It was a large group of Mississippi State fans. They'd seen what was going on and were coming to the rescue. They weren't confrontational at all. In fact, they shook hands and slapped the guys on the back and said, "Why don't you come with us? We'll buy you a beer." It was the perfect way to calm things down and rescue a few damsels in distress.

As the group of maroon and blue moved away, one of the Mississippi State fans turned and winked at me. I mouthed the words, "Thank you," and turned back to Shannon. And while I know not to judge an entire group of people by the actions of a few, I will always have a soft spot in my heart for Mississippi State.

We lost to Kentucky that day, but as near as I remember, nobody drew blood.

24 Tornado

L IKE Aries, Shannon has always been afraid of thunderstorms. As a result, she is a bit obsessed with weather patterns. She watches the weather on the news, checks it online, has a weather app on her phone ... she keeps up. And sometimes, she frets.

One stormy night when Joey was still in high school, Shannon was being particularly fretful, worrying about tornado watches that were in effect for us and several surrounding counties. I was working at the computer in my bedroom, and finally I told her to just go to bed and stop worrying about it. It was going to be fine. It was just a bit of rain.

About twenty minutes later, sitting at my computer, I felt the hairs stand up on the back of my neck and I was seized with a sudden sense of impending doom.

"Shannon?" I called out, trying to keep my voice as calm as possible. "Why don't you come back in here with me?"

I had barely gotten the words out of my mouth, when it started. My entire house began shaking, rocking back and forth, rattling things off shelves. As my belongings crashed to the floor, I ran to my bedroom door, meeting Shannon there.

I screamed for Joey, whose bedroom was on the other side of the house. I grabbed Shannon, pushed her to the floor, and threw myself on top of her, covering her with my body, still screaming for Joey.

As we were lying there amid all the noise and shaking, we heard an enormous whoosh and BOOM! Something slammed against the wall next to my head, and I realized that my washer and dryer were on the other side of the wall.

"Great," I thought. "I try to protect Shannon, and I put her in the one spot in the house that is the most likely to get her crushed to death."

I could hear Joey yelling in the house behind me somewhere and the noise and shaking subsided as suddenly as it had begun.

I was still lying on top of Shannon, spread-eagled on our bathroom floor. Joey was standing over us, excitedly asking if we were ok.

From somewhere beneath me, we heard a muffled voice.

"I was right!" Shannon said, face-down with her mother on top of her, but still determined to say, "I told you so."

I started laughing. Laughing at my hilarious daughter and laughing for joy that we were all ok. In fact, I was laughing so hard I could barely get up off the floor. Joey had to give me a hand up.

And then I stopped laughing. Because I remembered about Aries. He was out there. Was he ok?

Years before, when we were still boarding at Bar M, several horses were struck and killed by a bolt of lightning. I was the unofficial barn photographer and always had my camera with me. (This was before everyone had cell phones, with their built-in cameras that record everything.) Gay asked me to take photos of the dead horses, for insurance purposes, before they buried them all. It was one favor I wish I'd turned down. Because the images of those poor horses, scattered around the ground, was burned into my brain forever. And although I wasn't particularly afraid of bad weather myself, it always made me a bit terrified for Aries.

And so I was suddenly *very* terrified. So much so that my brain fogged over. I dashed to the kitchen door and pulled it open. Somehow, I found myself flung back against my refrigerator, and for a moment, I thought it was that weird unequal pressure thing that people talk about in tornadoes. I've heard that houses can literally explode during a tornado, because of the unequal pressure, and for years I would open a couple of windows just a crack, whenever tornadoes were threatened. I didn't want my house exploding.

But then I realized that it wasn't the pressure. There were tree branches pushing me back. The tornado had dropped a tree onto my deck and the branches had been pushing against the door. When I turned the knob to open the door, those branches had sprung into my kitchen, pushing the door open and flinging me against the refrigerator like a rag doll.

And I became even more terrified. I started to climb out through those limbs. Joey grabbed me, trying to hold me back. I screamed at him, shaking him off. I had to see if Aries was ok. I scrambled out through the branches, onto my deck and ran out into the rain and darkness, barefoot as usual.

Trees and debris littered the ground. The tree on my deck was enormous and I could see another one that had fallen between my house and my garage. I strained my eyes, looking for that familiar white shape through the rain.

I started down toward his stall, and finally spotted him, standing in the middle of his pasture. Upright. Four legs squarely under him, no visible sign of distress or injury. Wet, but otherwise ok. I breathed a sigh of relief.

And then the wind began to pick up again, and I became afraid again … this time for me. What was I thinking, running out barefoot into a tornado? Tornadoes often moved in packs. I knew that … I was from Arkansas, for heaven's sake!

And then I heard a zzzt-zzzt sort of sound and realized that there were power lines down somewhere in my yard. And I was barefoot. How stupid could I get?

I turned and walked back toward the house, forcing myself to go slowly enough that I could look where I was putting each foot. It seemed to take forever to reach the deck, and the wind was blowing so hard, I thought it was going to rip my t-shirt right off me.

And then I was presented with another problem. Aided by adrenaline, my scramble through the tree branches out seemed quick and easy. Getting back in wasn't so easy. Aside from the adrenaline issue, it seemed I was climbing along with the branches on the way out. The way back in, branches were facing toward me, grabbing onto me and thwarting my attempts.

Joey was still standing in the doorway and spotted me. He reached out one arm, and I reached up and clasped his wrist. And he basically dragged me back into the house, tree branches clawing into my arms and legs. I was reminded of the scene from *Poltergeist*, where the tree tries to eat the kid, and his dad drags him out.

Rain was pouring into the kitchen through the open door and the wind was horrendous, but we couldn't shut the door because of the branches. I found a hand saw and Joey had to quickly saw off several of the larger branches and then forced the door shut.

Then he turned to me, grabbed me by the shoulders and bent down, looking right into my face. "Mom, I love you," he said, "But don't you ever do anything that stupid again, ok?"

The next day, we went out to survey the damage. The tree that had landed on my deck had taken off a few shingles on its way down. And in addition to the tree that I had seen between my house and garage the night before, there was also another one down in my back yard. I basically had a ring of trees around my house, but miraculously, none of them had done any real damage to my house.

Aries was fine as well, not a scratch on him. His fence had been torn away in huge sections, but he had stayed put, apparently not even tempted to venture out of the safety of his pasture.

25 Ebb and Flow

KATIE was coming home. Not to my house, but to the Atlanta area. She had traveled all over, working in Virginia, California, Canada, New Jersey ... she'd even spent some time in Europe, working on a horse farm in Belgium. She'd rubbed elbows with the rich and famous, working for one Olympic team member and running into all kinds of celebrities.

One day, I was standing at the break table at FC&A, flipping through a *People* magazine, when I spotted a photo of Bruce Springsteen standing next to a little girl on a pony. The caption said something about Bruce being with his daughter at a horse show in Wellington, Florida.

"Huh," I thought. "Katie is at a horse show in Wellington right now." I dropped the magazine, went straight to my office and dialed her number.

As soon as she said, "Hello," I said, "Katie, have you seen Bruce Springsteen?"

Her answer? "Not today." NOT TODAY?

"So you have seen him," I was trying to remain calm.

"Well, yeah. His daughter has a pony down here."

"I know. I saw it in *People* magazine!" I think Katie was beginning to pick up on my excitement.

"You know, Princess Ann's daughter is here too," she said, "So we see her all the time."

Princess Ann, Schmincess Ann. My daughter had laid eyes on Bruce freakin' Springsteen. For free.

But nothing topped the time she met Robin Williams (my biggest celebrity crush) in California and got him to autograph a photo for me. That photo still sits on my kitchen counter, with the inscription: "To Tammy, All my love, Robin." It is one of my most cherished possessions, silly as it may seem.

But I would much rather have my daughter nearby than meeting celebrities in far away places, so I was thrilled that she was coming home. She got a job managing a hunter/jumper facility in Atlanta, and soon met her husband-to-be.

But not everything was coming up roses for me. For most people, myself included, life is not a rags to riches story. It's not a steady climb or descent. Life ebbs and flows. The good and the bad. The yin and the yang.

My particular life's flow seemed to always center around exhaustion. In looking back, it's funny how often the word "exhausted" could be used to describe me. Most of it was self-imposed. I considered it the highest compliment for someone to refer to me as "hard-working." I was stubborn, and I would push my body to the breaking limit to keep a roof over our heads or to help my kids out. But whenever I punished my body like that, it punished me back. By messing with my brain.

"Hah!" my body would say. "Think you can make me subsist on three hours of sleep a night, or stay up for 48 hours straight? Think you can work me until my every muscle aches and screams? Watch this. I'll impair your brain function and force you to act in ridiculous ways and make stupendously stupid decisions."

And so it was, sometime in Joey's freshman year in college, I quit school for the second time, after earning a pretty much worthless Associate's Degree, and only a few classes short of getting a Bachelor's degree that might have been a bit more marketable.

Joey had unfortunately inherited my family's tendency to gain weight. His body looked more like a football player than a basketball player, and so he was required to do extra conditioning. Make no mistake, the normal regimen of conditioning at an SEC school is grueling. It pushes conditioned athletes to their limits. That's what it is supposed to do. But take someone like Joey, who isn't in the best condition, and have them do that, plus even more, and it becomes almost physically impossible.

Also, he was away from home for the first time, had to keep up with his classes, and was performing in plays, as that was a requirement for his degree. And it was his passion, the same as basketball. His passions collided, however, as finding time to fulfill his basketball commitments and his theatre commitments proved difficult.

This confluence of conditions led to physical manifestations, the most disturbing of which were seizures. Oddly, Joey was experiencing seizure activity on only the left side of his body. His muscles would begin twitching involuntarily, and he would find it difficult to walk, because he would lose control over his left leg.

As Joey became hospitalized on several occasions, I began to drive to Athens several times a week, which was almost three hours each way. It was almost like working two full-time jobs again.

And so, in the throes of fatigue and stress, I quit my job. My dream job. I still refer to it was "the second worst decision of my life."

I had freelance work, I reasoned. If I had time to work on my freelance, I could build that business up and wouldn't even need a full time job. I could stay home with Shannon and Aries, have time to take care of Joey, and everything would be sunshine and unicorns. Except that it was more like a monsoons and monsters.

I had picked the worst time possible to try to build a freelance business up. While I always had some work coming in, the economy was taking a downturn. Clients were going out of business. Work was harder to find, rather than easier.

Then I made yet another stupid decision. I got my realtor's license. My timing was impeccable. It preceded the terrible housing crash. Established realtors and builders were going under right and left. Foreclosures were everywhere, and no one was buying. Financing was much tougher to get as mortgage companies tightened standards they should have tightened years before.

Not only was I unable to sell houses, I had spent a lot of money trying to establish myself. And then of course, I began to struggle to pay my own mortgage as my rate adjusted up and up, and my income went down and down.

Worse than that, I began to lose my support system. I lost touch with many of my long-time friends from FC&A, although the company would continue to support me with freelance projects for years to come.

And worst of all, my menagerie, my delightful band of critters, was slowly being whittled down.

Twinkie had passed away, and then my Hooch, my brilliant friend and most stalwart protector, gave in to his advancing age.

Not a week after losing Hooch, Deb colicked and passed away in my pasture. He was 18 years old. He had a good life. My brother had loved him and cared for him, and then I had done the same. He and Aries had become great, inseparable friends. He would be missed.

My sweet Pixel held on for a couple more years, but she developed mammary cancer, and I had to make that drive to the vet that I always seem to choose to make in the middle of the night. Past Rock House, where she'd accompanied me on countless walks in the pasture, being rewarded with a splash in the lake at the end. There wasn't much Pixel enjoyed more than getting muddy. Except gnawing gently on my arm while I stroked her silky ears and she gazed into my eyes with adoration.

It is inevitable, the loss and the grief that comes with caring for creatures with shorter life spans than ours. Sometimes, it hurts so much, we question whether it's worth it. We question it, even though we know the answer.

Thank God I still had Aries. My rock. My inspiration.

I went back to my blue-collar roots and got a job waiting tables at Smokey Bones, a barbeque restaurant in Peachtree City. Within a couple of months, I became a bartender there and discovered that I enjoyed it immensely. Many of the same people came in day after day, week after week, and I got to know them. One of my favorite couples, Al and Maggie, were both retired military and enjoyed traveling the world. I loved hearing their stories and seeing the photos they'd taken in all kinds of places.

And as the recession deepened and foreclosures rates skyrocketed, I continued to cling stubbornly to my little piece of dirt in the middle of nowhere.

I heard there were government programs that offered assistance to people who were in foreclosure, but found that you had to be even further behind in your mortgage payments than I was. Many people I knew stopped even trying to pay their mortgage, and I was given that advice as well. If I got far enough behind, I might qualify for a bail out. If I didn't, well, I should just try to save the money that I would have been paying on my mortgage, so that I'd have enough money to go rent an apartment somewhere for Shan and me, once I was evicted. But if I did that, if I gave up on my home, what would happen to Aries? I had promised myself (and him) that we would be together until the end, so I had to do whatever I could to hold on.

So of course, I worked. And worked. And I applied for a loan modification that would refinance my mortgage to a lower, fixed rate of interest that I could afford. My mortgage company gave me a probationary period, and my understanding was that if I could make my full payments on time for six months, they would grant the modification. However, at the end of the six months, they said I had to do it for *another* six months. One mis-entered number (by their representative) and they said I was in default and I got the notice that I had to move out.

And yet, I wouldn't give up. I wrote an overly passionate but apparently persuasive letter to my mortgage company, detailing my resolve and pointing out that, given the current market, if they evicted me, it could be years before they found another person to buy the property. A bird in the hand, as they say...

And miracle of miracles, they conceded. I got my refinance. I got a fixed rate. I got a lower monthly payment. The bad part was that, after paying on my mortgage for more than 10 years, I suddenly had another 30 years before it would be paid off. The mortgage company wins, after all. They always do.

But I didn't care. Shannon, Aries and I were safe in the Middle of Nowhere.

26 Heroes

I still hadn't found a regular vet for Aries who came close to replacing Johnny Pritchard, when Aries experienced another colic episode. I'd already had one bad experience with the same crazy vet who'd treated Deb's eye, in which she told me that "Arabians were just big babies, and couldn't take pain" and "horse owners think their horse is colicking every time he lies down."

And so we were trying yet another new vet. Shannon and I were standing in the yard, with Aries on a lead. I had brought him into the yard, under our flood lights, because it was close to sundown. We heard the truck turn into the driveway, and in a moment, it came into view. It had a license plate on the front with a big orange "T" on it.

Next to me, I heard Shannon draw a deep breath. "Ugh," she said. "I think he's a Tennessee fan."

He pulled up, rolled his window down and began to ask me about Aries, when Shannon interrupted.

"Hey!" she said, her head cocked to one side and her finger pointing in a vaguely accusatory manner. "Are you a Tennessee fan?"

I held my breath and watched his face closely. He looked at Shannon, and smiled broadly. "Go Vols!" he said. "Are *you* a Tennessee fan?"

"Ugh! No! I think I'm a Bulldog fan!" Shannon preceded almost all her sentences with "I think," no matter how sure she was of the statement. And there wasn't much she could have said with more certainty. She was definitely a Bulldog fan.

He laughed and asked her a question about the Bulldogs current football coach, Mark Richt, which she followed up with a statement about the Volunteers' current players. And that, as they say, was the start of a beautiful friendship.

Dr. Matt's treatment of Aries was professional and spot on, and he'd passed the Shannon test with flying colors. I felt relieved that perhaps I'd found "the one." His real test, however, would come a few weeks later.

I still had the habit of visiting Aries in the middle of the night when I couldn't sleep, but one night, I was sleeping soundly, when I suddenly sat bolt upright in bed. Something was wrong with Aries. I just knew it. I flung the covers off and went outside, not bothering to put on shoes or anything. I walked out onto my deck and looked for him. He wasn't up by the fence near the house, so I called his name. Out of the darkness, I heard a responding nicker, and I relaxed. He was ok.

I waited a couple of minutes, straining my eyes into the darkness to see his white form appear, but nothing happened. That was odd. Aries always came when I called. I called again, and again heard him respond, but still he didn't appear. So I went out to the pasture, hobbling over my gravel driveway, unlatched his gate, and walked into his pasture. I called again, and he answered, and I moved in the direction of the sound.

Finally, I saw him, standing stock still about midway down the fence line, next to a stand of young trees. He saw me too, but he still wasn't coming toward me. This was very strange behavior for him, but I was trying not to panic. I could always tell when he was colicking, just by looking at his face, but I didn't see that look now. His ears were pricked forward and his eyes were clear. He seemed fine. He just wasn't moving.

I looked him all over, but didn't see anything wrong. Of course, I hadn't brought a flashlight with me, so I went back into the house to get one.

I also got a small scoop of feed, an apple, a halter and lead line, and my cell phone. And I slipped my feet into my garden clogs and headed back out.

I approached Aries, and offered him the apple, holding it just out of his reach. He stretched his neck out as far as it would go, but refused to take even one step forward to get it. I did the same with the feed, putting it in his feed pan just out of his reach. He leaned down and stretched his neck out, popping his lips together in anticipation, but still would not move his legs.

My heart sank. Maybe he had a broken leg. Everyone knows what happens to horses who break a leg.

I shined the flashlight over every inch of his body, but still didn't see anything amiss. No protruding bones, no odd angles to his limbs. Just his usual stance, with his unusual refusal to budge, even for food.

I stuck my flashlight between my knees and began to run my hands down each of his legs. I had no idea what I was looking for, but I'd repeated this motion thousands of times while bathing him, using my hands as a squeegee to whisk the excess water from his legs. If anything felt different, I thought I'd at least notice it.

But still nothing. And then as I finished my examination of his right hind leg, in the dim glow of the flashlight, I watched a tiny drop of blood strike the inside of his hoof. I bent over, took my flashlight from its knee hold, and shined it upward onto Aries' belly.

I was horrified to see a branch, about an inch or two in diameter, sticking out of his groin area. He'd been impaled somehow. I fought down the rising panic in my gut and grabbed the stick and pulled to see if I could pull it out. When I did, a rivulet of blood began to run down the stick, dripping onto the ground. I stopped. If I pulled it out, he might bleed to death. I had no idea how deep it had gone or what injuries it might have caused. I knew that it must be in pretty deep, because it didn't pull out easily.

With shaking hands, I flipped open my cell phone and dialed my new vet's number. It was 2 a.m.

He was sleepy. You could tell. And he was not happy to hear my hysterical voice. He had just gotten home from another emergency call. He had made it to his bed, but not yet to sleep. He didn't want to get back up and go to work. And especially not for a crazy lady he'd only met once who couldn't say anything but, "He has a stick stuck in his groin." And, "You have to come. You HAVE to come! PLEASE!"

He told me just to pull it out. I told him I tried. I tried to describe the horror to him. But I was already thinking of what I should do when he told me he couldn't come. Try to find another vet? Nobody would come. Wait until morning? Try harder to pull it out? I'd need to gather some clean cloths for stanching the massive blood flow I was sure would ensue. And alcohol. He'd need disinfection.

Then I heard a heavy sigh on the other end of the line, and I felt a glimmer of hope. "I'll be there in twenty minutes." Another heavy sigh. "Please have him up by the lights in your yard. Where you had him before."

I babbled a couple of thank yous and hung up.

Then I realized that it was going to be hard to get Aries out of the darkness of his pasture and into the light, when he wouldn't take a step. I put his halter on him and pulled. Still he refused to move an inch. His feet were stubbornly planted.

So I pulled out my cell phone again and called Katie. She was also asleep, but when your mother calls you at 2 a.m., you typically answer. I shakily explained the entire situation to her and then my problem. How was I to get him into the light if he wouldn't move?

"Mom," she said, "If Aries doesn't want to move, don't try to make him move. Trust him. The vet will understand."

I let her go back to sleep with a promise to text her any news.

When Dr. Matt arrived, I explained to him why I didn't have Aries where he'd asked. But I had flashlights. Shannon always has a collection of flashlights. She's a bit obsessed with them. Probably because she's afraid of the dark. She gets one for every birthday and Christmas. Different kinds, shapes and colors. Plus, I told him, I'd be happy to drive my truck into the pasture and use my headlights.

Matt said he thought the flashlight I had would work fine, and he didn't seem mad that he had to walk into the pasture.

He bent over to examine Aries. When he actually saw it, he understood why I was so freaked out. "What in the world?" he said, "How'd he do this?"

I didn't know, and was a little disappointed that this wasn't a common situation that they teach vets about in vet school. Apparently, horses impaling themselves with sticks in their groin areas wasn't a course offering.

"Before we do anything else, I need to palpate him. That stick looks like it's pretty far in there. If it's perforated his intestines, this might be it for him." A perforated intestine meant a slow, agonizing, painful death, so of course the only option at that point would be euthanasia.

My head spun. Matt put his glove on, and I moved toward Aries' head. I held his halter, pressed my forehead against his face, and I prayed. Hard.

After a few long moments, Matt spoke, not to me, but to Aries. "Well, old boy, you may have dodged the bullet with this one." Miraculously, Matt said, the stick seemed to have penetrated nothing but fatty tissue. An inch in one direction, and that night could have been his last. But it had entered just to the inside of his right hind leg, next to his sheath. If he had tried to walk, however ... if he had done what I had repeatedly urged him to do, that stick could have shifted and perhaps done irreparable damage. Thankfully, Aries was smarter than me. And Katie was smart enough to tell me to trust him.

Now we just had to get the stick out. Matt tried pulling it out with one hand but couldn't. So I held the flashlight for him, so he could grasp it with both hands. He braced himself and pulled mightily. The stick made a horrible sucking noise as it exited Aries' belly.

I expected a ton of blood, but oddly enough, there wasn't much at all. Dr. Matt applied disinfectant, gave me some antibiotics to head off any chance of infection, and left me with instructions to hose it off daily and keep an eye on the wound for any sign of infection. He handed me the stick and asked if I wanted to save it. I turned and gave it a mighty heave into the woods.

Matt shook his head as he left. "Well, this was a new one on me," he said. "I'll always remember this visit for sure."

So would I. I would remember it as an example of what an extraordinary vet does for his clients. Forgoes sleep. Trudges happily (or even grumpily) into overgrown pastures. Deals with semi-hysterical owners with sensitivity. Forget the knight in shining armor. A vet with a big orange "T" on his truck would do just fine.

27 Aging

Somehow, Aries had become a "senior" horse. It happens. You turn around, and one day the chubby toddler you remember is towering over you. The little girl who hid behind your legs is all dressed up and going to prom. The clumsy puppy who rode in the tiny space between your back seat and your rear window becomes gray and grizzled.

The average lifespan of a horse is 20 years. So once a horse is in his late teens, he's pretty much considered a senior. But Aries was extremely healthy for his age, and didn't seem to experience any arthritis at all.

I attributed that to his daily stretching ritual. Aries began that ritual when he was still young. Whenever he exited his stall at Rock House in the morning, he would pause in the aisle way. First, he would rock back on his hindquarters, stretching both forelegs out in front of him and bowing his neck down. Then, he would straighten up, and lift one hind leg up, stretch it out behind him and shake it. Then he would lift the other hind leg, stretch it out behind him and shake it. One last toss of his head, and he was ready to go. Slap a terrycloth headband and some leggings on him and he could have passed for Richard Simmons.

The other horses in the barn were not so crazy about his ritual during morning turn out. The ones who were in stalls behind him would be blocked in the narrow aisle, while he calmly stretched it out. They would weave back and forth and make impatient snorting noises, but Aries didn't seem to notice. He was completely chill, but they never tried to interrupt him or go around.

Even after leaving Rock House, Aries continued his stretching routine. Usually, he would do it whenever he got up from sleeping.

Although Aries was healthy and energetic for his age, horses, like people, almost always develop some health problems later in life, and one he developed was allergies. Every spring, he would break out in hives. Huge bumps would pop up all over his body. The first time it happened, Matt came out and examined him and gave me medicine for it. Every year after that, however, I would just call and say, "Aries has hives" and I could stop by the office and pick up his medicine. Once, Matt even met Joey in Senoia to give him the medicine, to save us a drive to Newnan.

This predisposition to itchiness finally helped me figure out how Aries had impaled himself that night. Because I wasn't able to keep his pasture mowed and cleared like I should, it was becoming overgrown with blackberry bushes and lots of small saplings.

Aries was an extremely resourceful creature, and had figured out how to scratch himself, using those little saplings. He would position himself just so, and then move around, using the tree as a scratching post. While he was doing this, something must have frightened him. Some horses, when startled, will react by doing this funny squatting thing, where they sort of hunker down. I guess they're getting their legs gathered underneath them, because they don't know which direction the danger is coming from. They want to be prepared for flight in any direction. I think that Aries must have gotten frightened in the middle of a good scratch, done that little startled squat maneuver, and impaled himself. It could have been much, much worse, however. Because what he was scratching was his sheath.

Owners of geldings know that you have to clean a horse's sheath regularly. It's not a pleasant job and involves gloves and lubrication. Or you can call the vet out, have him sedate your horse and do it. So of course, I called Matt.

At some point, I stopped riding Aries, but not because he was incapable. Mostly because I was also getting older and I *did* have arthritis. Also, I had gained back a lot of the weight I had lost all those years before.

I can't remember the last ride. I wish I could. But the truth is, we often don't remember the last time we do something, because we're unaware that it will *be* the last time. I imagine it was a short ride, bareback, with a halter. Maybe we went on a jaunt through the trails behind my house. More likely, we just rode around the yard for a few minutes, and then I let him graze, while I stretched out along his back and relaxed in the sun.

At any rate, I don't think he cared. I still spent time with him every day, just hanging out. He had worked so hard most of his life, being a lesson horse and taking care of us all, that he deserved his retirement. He seemed content and so was I.

He had developed a bad habit, though. One Katie thoroughly disapproved of, but I indulged him anyway. He enjoyed scratching his head on my shoulder. I would brace myself, and he would rub his forehead up and down along my shoulder. He did do it rather hard, and I could see how it might be a problem if he tried to do that to a small child. It was kind of the equivalent of letting your dog jump on you. It might not bother you, but if he jumps on someone else … someone small or elderly … he could hurt them. That's why you don't let your dog jump on you.

But Aries was now a senior horse, and he never went anywhere, and there wasn't much chance of a small or elderly person popping up in his pasture. He enjoyed his head scratch, and I didn't mind, so it was ok.

Then one day, I was cleaning out his water trough. I dumped it out, filled it halfway with more water and was scrubbing away at the slimy green algae that seems to form overnight.

Aries spotted my upturned hindquarters and decided that my large jean-clad butt would be an even more excellent scratching post than my shoulder. I never saw him coming. Imagine my surprise when I found myself pushed head first into that slimy green water. Cold water. I tried hard not to swallow any of it, but probably inhaled about a quart of it as I gasped with shock. I rolled over, lying there fully clothed and wet as if I were in a bathtub. (Actually, it was a bathtub. Michelle's father had sealed up the drain and it served as a perfectly good water trough for years.)

And of course, Aries was blinking down at me with complete innocence and surprise. "Why, whatever do you think you're doing in my water trough?"

I went inside to change my clothes, and promised myself that I would never admit to Katie that she was right. Again.

* * *

One of the challenges with senior horses is that they tend to lose weight. Most often, this is because of their teeth. They can no longer chew their food well enough to properly digest it. This also increases the danger of colic, as half-chewed food is more likely to accumulate in their gut and cause an impaction.

Since Aries was already prone to colic, I worried about this. I had already begun feeding him a special feed formulated for senior horses, but as he aged, I would also begin to soak his food. I had a big orange bowl that was supposed to be a chip bowl. I would fill that bowl up with feed, add water and let it soak before I fed it to him. That way, I knew he was getting more moisture in his system, and I didn't have to worry about him not chewing his food up properly. He didn't seem to mind this change, probably because I also cut up apples and carrots into it, to give him a little variety. As he grew even older, I would begin to grate the carrots, because I was worried that they were too hard and he might choke on them.

I also bought him alfalfa hay, because it seemed as if he was more likely to colic when he ate Bermuda. Bermuda was the most common kind of hay in Georgia, and the cheapest. But it is sort of a fine cut grain and has more of a tendency to clump together during digestion. Alfalfa is a coarser grain, so it provides more roughage. Also, it's more nutritionally dense than Bermuda, so I felt like it was better for him. I would order a hundred bales of alfalfa at a time from a guy in Kentucky, and he would deliver to my house, and help me stack it in my garage.

A horse person will lift thousands of bales of hay in his or her lifetime. And thousands of 50-pound bags of feed. I have picked up hay in fields numerous times, tossing the bales onto a moving trailer. But as I grew older and more sedentary, it was funny how much heavier fifty pounds became.

My solemn vow to Sam, all those years before, that Aries and I would grow old and toothless together was coming true. And it was glorious.

28 CLONES

MY new job, like my old job, was located in Peachtree City. Peachtree City is a planned community, criss-crossed by miles of golf cart paths. It has regularly been ranked by *Money* magazine as one of the "100 Best Places to Live in the United States." It is ideal for retirement age folks, thanks in part to all those golf cart paths. You can get anywhere in PTC on a golf cart. Most of the parking lots have special tiny spaces designated just for them.

Peachtree City boasts an extremely vigilant and competent police force, it's family-oriented, and it has a small amphitheater that attracts mostly older acts that were popular when I was growing up ... The Monkees, Cheap Trick, The B52s, Rick Springfield ... even the legendary BB King played there. Peachtree City is quiet, calm, and decidedly affluent. And it is so different from the surrounding areas, that people came to refer to it as "The Bubble."

It was the perfect place for me to be a bartender. I rarely had to deal with obnoxious drunks, and I worked mostly day shift, so most of my clientele was my age or older. I served more martinis and Manhattans than Jaeger bombs and Jello shots. Most of the other bartenders (ok, ALL the other bartenders) were youngsters in their early 20s. But I think I provided a nice change of pace for the retired folk in Peachtree City. Part of being a bartender is being able to converse comfortably with all kinds of people, and I admit that was outside my comfort zone. But a girl's gotta do whatever it takes to keep a roof over her head and hay in the garage.

So I talked to people. Actually, mostly I listened. I found I didn't have a lot in common with most of my guests. I wasn't well-versed in sports talk, so I typically just quoted Shannon. If she was lamenting an injury or a trade of one of her favorite players, I could work that into conversation and trust that she hadn't given me a bum steer.

When people did manage to suck me into a two-way conversation, the topic that most often came up was, of course, Aries. It was what set me apart from everyone else. They might have more money and education than me, they might be well-read and well-traveled, but I had the most beautiful horse in the world. Nobody could top that.

But as I talked about Aries, a disturbing trend emerged. People would ask me how old he was. When I would respond that he was 28 or 29 or 30, they would pause, usually frowning just a little. And the follow-up question was invariably, "How long do horses live?"

My answer to that became a pat and emphatic, "This one is going to live FOREVER."

Usually, that was enough to deter people from that line of questioning, but one day, one of my regular guests decided to persist. So I told him that the average life span was about 20, but that horses, like people, were beginning to live longer and longer. I had heard of a horse in England that was thought to be in his fifties. I was hoping Aries would break that record. I told him that if Aries went, they'd just have to dig the hole a little deeper, because they'd have to put me in there, too. I simply couldn't imagine life without him.

And this guy could see my distress. But rather than change the subject, like most people, he kept on. Because he was a problem solver by nature – an army engineer.

"Can you breed him?" he asked. "Then at least you'd have his babies."

"No," I said. "He's a gelding … he's been neutered."

"What about cloning?" he asked.

This was a new one. I hadn't thought of that.

"It's been probably 20 years since they cloned that sheep. Surely they're cloning horses by now."

I was suddenly excited beyond measure. I'd always regretted the fact that I couldn't have an Aries baby, and this guy had dropped a possibility bomb into my lap.

I called Katie on the way home. I couldn't wait to get to a computer, and she'd know.

She told me that yes, they did clone horses. In fact, they had cloned Gem Twist, an Olympic show jumper and one of my favorite "celebrity" horses of all time.

I was perhaps particularly fond of Gem Twist because he reminded me of Aries. They looked remarkably similar, although Aries, of course, had the edge of being the most beautiful horse in the world.

Katie even knew the name of the company that handled the cloning. But she also heard the excitement in my voice and tried to talk me down.

"Mom, it wouldn't *be* Aries, you know."

"I know, I know. But it would be something *of* him." The idea of having a miniature Aries that I could raise and love and mold was just sending me over the moon. Almost as good as having a grandbaby.

When I got home, Google revealed good news and bad news. The process of cloning horses was viable and established. Not only were Gem Twist's clones alive and healthy, they were intact. They were stallions, capable of breeding. His first clone was named Gemini, which I found incredibly clever. Gemini now has offspring that are grown and ready to compete. They will probably never measure up to Gem Twist, and I knew that an Aries clone would never measure up to him in my eyes, but still …

The bad news, however, was really bad. The cost was, to say the least, prohibitive. Something like $85,000 prohibitive. For a bartender/free-lancer, that was pie in the sky.

Still, you never know what could happen, so I tucked the cloning information away in my memory banks, and focused on what I did best. Working.

Since leaving FC&A, I no longer had health insurance. Or sick days. Or paid holidays. So when I dropped a crate of sodas on my foot and broke my toe, I didn't go to the doctor. I didn't get x-rays, but, with all the broken bones I've had in my life, I knew it was broken.

It swelled up so badly that it wouldn't fit in my shoe. So I took an old pair of black shoes, cut half the top off of it, giving my swollen toe room to fit, wore black socks so it wouldn't be so obvious, and off to work I went.

Then the toe became infected. The infection was under the toenail, however. When Shannon was little, she accidentally shut her finger in a car door, and she had the same kind of infection under her fingernail. The doctor told me that they had to take the fingernail off, so the infection could drain. Otherwise, it might get into her bone, and then we'd have to amputate her finger. Scary. So of course, I let them sedate her and remove the fingernail. Even with sedation, she screamed. Cut me right to the core. But it was for her own good.

And that's how I knew that my toenail had to come off. I armed myself with some heavy-duty toenail clippers and a pair of pliers and went to work. I had to do it a little at a time, giving myself a break from the pain occasionally.

Shannon sat on the edge of the bed and watched. She was fascinated by all things medical. Her obsession with Major League Baseball's disabled list was one indication of that. When we were first able to afford cable TV, I would often come home to find her watching an "operation" channel, where you could observe surgeries being performed. Or she'd be watching "Smurfs." If there wasn't any baseball on, of course.

So there was no question that she had to watch the whole process. She would lean forward, inspecting my progress closely. Then, overcome by all the blood and green ooze, she would lean back, avert her eyes and say, "Ugh!" After a few seconds, however, she'd lean in again. It was hilarious, and the laughter she provided was a wonderful anesthetic.

Then Joey happened to come in for a visit from college. He had left the basketball team after his second year to focus on academics and was much happier and healthier. But when he walked in and saw me sitting there with a pair of pliers, blood everywhere, he was shocked.

"Jesus Christ, Mom! What are you doing?"

"It's infected," I said. "I have to take the toenail off."

"Then go to a doctor!"

"Son, I don't have the money," I replied.

Joey stood there a second, and then turned and punched a hole in wall behind him in frustration.

And I bandaged my toe, put my half-a-shoe on and went to work.

I still haven't patched that hole in the wall.

29 Cowboys

I had always yearned to see more of the world, but I had jetsetter dreams on a carpool budget. Ever since Katie had grown up, however, she had tried to get me out of my tiny circle in Georgia whenever she could. She took me to New Orleans for my fortieth birthday. She flew me to New York, just for the day, just so I could see it and say I'd been there.

When she was working in Wellington, Florida, near West Palm Beach, she got me a plane ticket to come visit her, and then arranged for us to take a hydrofoil over to the Bahamas for a day with some of her friends. That particular trip proved memorable for both of us and embarrassing for me, as I accidentally consumed too much rum and became quite outgoing and entertaining. I had never so much as drank a beer in front of any of my children at the time, but lulled by the warm sunshine and the laid-back Caribbean atmosphere, I overindulged. And apparently, I told stories about Aries to anyone who would listen to me. And after a couple of minutes, I would repeat the same stories. She and her friends were saints for putting up with me. Even so, it was a wonderful day. The stuff life is made of. And stories that you'll never live down.

After my first grandbaby was born, and I was up to my elbows in grammy heaven, Katie and her husband presented me with a gift. It was a guidebook to the Hawaiian Islands.

"Oh wow. Thanks," I said, secretly slightly puzzled by the gift.

"You're going to need that, because we're taking you to Hawaii with us," Katie said.

I couldn't believe it. Me. In Hawaii. I had visions of Tom Selleck on a beach in his 70s short shorts and tube socks and me in a sarong, ukuleles playing in the background.

But before I could fly off to paradise for a week, I had to figure out what to do with Shannon and all my critters. Shannon wasn't fond of flying, and opted to stay with her cousin Amanda, so I didn't have to worry too much about her. Joey promised to look after my dogs, but I was worried about Aries.

He'd been alone since we lost Deb, but he seemed happy. Still, I didn't like the idea of him there by himself for a whole week without me. So I called Katie's friend Lisa.

Lisa and Katie had met at Rock House, years before, and now Lisa owned her own boarding facility, Iron Gate Farm, which was only a few minutes from my house. I arranged for Aries to stay with Lisa for a month, as I wanted him to have time to settle in there before I left him to fly away with Tom Selleck.

Lisa was duly impressed with Aries' beauty and personality. She confided in me that she usually wasn't that fond of Arabians, but Aries was just so sweet ...

Aries did create a little problem at Iron Gate, however. He fell head over heels in love with a sassy little vixen of a paint mare. He couldn't stand for her to be out of his sight. Lisa called and told me that she couldn't turn Scarlett out and leave him in his stall or he'd start acting crazy. She was afraid he'd hurt himself.

I thought Lisa was surely exaggerating, so I had to go see for myself. When I arrived, he was grazing contentedly near a paint mare that I had to admit was rather cute. He was perfectly cooperative when I went to put his halter on him, pausing for a moment so he could scratch his head on my shoulder. I looked at Lisa with a slightly red face. "Katie hates it when he does this."

"Well....," she said.

And I said, "I know. I know." And let him finish scratching.

Then I took him inside and put him in his stall. He followed me in, no problem. I took his halter off, stepped outside and closed the door. Suddenly, big problem.

First he just looked at me hard and whinnied. Trumpeted would be more of an apt description. Insistent. Maybe even a little angry. "You don't think you're going to lock me in here and leave me do you?"

I stepped back, a little startled. "Oh my," I said.

"Just wait," Lisa said. "It gets worse."

And it did. My gentle, elderly Aries transformed before my very eyes. He bowed his neck and threw his chest out. He paced rapidly, anxiously, back and forth in the stall. And then he rocked back on his hindquarters, and his front legs came up off the ground. "Holy cow!" I thought. "He's going to try to jump out of the stall."

"Cut it out!" I scolded him. "You're THIRTY-TWO!" It was like watching a ninety-year-old man in a nursing home suddenly "hulk out" in defense of his lady love.

But his intention was clear. He was coming out of that stall one way or another. I quickly unlatched his door, and the second my hand touched the latch, he calmed down.

And so, for the remainder of his visit at Iron Gate, Aries was allowed to remain within eyesight of a certain black and white paint mare.

My vacation was indeed paradise, but once we touched down at Hartsfield International in Atlanta, I couldn't wait to get Aries home.

It was probably only a week or two after I returned from Hawaii that I found Aries down in his stall. He was colicking. The look on his face and the feeling in the pit of my stomach told me that this colic was different from the ones that came before. This one was a monster.

Dr. Matt came out and did the usual. Flushed him out, gave him Banamine, made him more comfortable. And told me to call him in the morning with an update.

I was in Aries' stall at the crack of dawn. And he was down again. In tears, I called Matt and asked him to come back out. I couldn't even get Aries to stand up, but Matt was a little rougher than I was, smacking him and prodding him into getting on his feet. But I could see how much effort it took for him.

Matt did his examination and then turned to me, that serious look on his face, and I knew what he was going to say. But all he got out was, "Tammy..." and I said, "No. No! There has to be something we can do. We can take him to Auburn."

"Tammy, you know they're not going to do surgery on a 32-year-old horse." His tone was gentle and his eyes were pained. I knew I should give in. I knew I should let him off the hook, but I couldn't. It wasn't time.

"There has to be something. Something."

"Well," he said, and with that "well" a determined light sprang up, growing from my gut and up into my throat. This wasn't "it." This couldn't be "it."

"I think the kind of colic he has is a nephrosplenic entrapment. His colon has gotten trapped between his spleen and his kidney. There is a method they use, where they give the horse a medication that causes all his internal organs to shrink temporarily. Then they jog the horse, and sometimes the motion enables the colon to slip back into place."

"Ok, then. Ok. We can do that."

"It's not 100% effective, and it can be hard on him, because it affects *all* his organs, not just his kidneys and spleen."

"So we could put him through all that, and he still might not make it?"

"There's no guarantee, and at his age, it's risky. But you have to make a decision quickly, because time is of the essence. The longer we wait, the less likely it is to work."

I looked at Aries, standing there with his head hanging, sedated heavily, and I just lost it. I didn't know what to do. So of course, I called Katie.

I sobbed hysterically into the phone. She was her usual calm self and Matt stood there patiently as his insane client talked on the phone to her daughter.

Katie managed to get most of the details out of me, and then asked me what she could do to help.

"Talk to my vet. I need you to talk to my vet!"

"Mom, do you need me to talk to your vet because you don't understand what he's telling you, or because you need help making a decision?"

"Both! Please, just talk to my vet!" I thrust my phone toward Matt, and turned back to Aries.

Matt explained everything to Katie, and then he handed the phone back to me.

"Ok, Mom," she said. "I think you should take Aries to Auburn. I'll pay for it if you need me to. But you need to *hurry*. This has already been going on for a while. I can come take him for you, but I won't be able to get there for three or four hours. Do you think Lisa can help?"

I told her if I couldn't figure out how to get Aries to Auburn, I'd call her back.

So Matt went on his way and I got on my phone.

The second Lisa answered, I said, "Do you feel like a trip to Auburn today?"

And bless her heart, she didn't hesitate a second. "Sure," she said, "What's going on?"

I explained the situation to her and she told me she would be there as quickly as possible. I called Katie back to tell her I'd found a ride to Auburn for Aries.

"How's he doing?" Katie asked.

"He's down again," I said.

"Ok. There's an old cowboy trick I want you to try. Take a couple of ropes and loop them around his legs and roll him over to the other side."

"Like when a horse is cast in his stall?" I asked.

"Yes. Exactly like that," she replied. "But you have to do it slowly. Because sometimes, that will allow the colon to slide out from between the kidney and the spleen and back into place."

Horses sometimes get "cast" in their stalls when they try to roll too close to a wall. Their legs hit the wall, and they are unable to generate enough momentum to flip themselves back over. So they're stuck, kind of like a turtle on its back. To help them upright themselves, you generally loop ropes over their front and back legs, high up, close to the body, and you pull. If you pull on the lower part of their legs, you could injure them. It's tougher to do when the ropes are up higher, because you don't have as much leverage, but it's much safer for the horse. Also, it is a two person job. It takes some muscle.

So I called Joey. But he couldn't get there quickly enough. It was up to Shannon and me.

I had two lead ropes. One was longer than the other, so I gave the longer one to Shannon. I looped the ropes around his legs and Shannon and I planted our feet in the dirt and pulled. Katie needn't have worried about us doing it too fast, because it was tough pulling him over. We strained mightily, and finally managed to flip him over. Because the lead I was using was a little too short, his hooves struck my leg on the way down, but I barely noticed the pain. Because it seemed to have had no effect on him. He still just lay there.

I sat beside him and waited for Lisa to arrive. I thought I heard her truck, but when it didn't appear for a few minutes, I walked down my driveway to look for her. What I saw made my heart sink into the gravel. Lisa's trailer was stuck in my driveway.

Lisa was already out, looking at the problem. My driveway was narrow, and she didn't have a lot of room to swing out in the road before turning, so one of the trailer wheels had gone into the ditch. The back of the trailer was sitting on the road, and the wheel was suspended in mid-air over the ditch.

My flicker of hope was flickering out, when Lisa looked at me and said, "I have a jack."

And it flickered back. We could do this. I had once put a fuel tank in a Ford Tempo. The two of us could surely get a horse trailer out of a ditch. So we gathered boards and blocks and built a tower for the jack to sit on so that it would reach the body of the trailer. It was a precarious tower, but once we got the trailer up high enough, I slid a piece of plywood across the ditch, under the wheel, effectively building a temporary bridge. But I told Lisa that bridge wasn't going to hold for long, once I let the jack down, so as soon as I gave her the word, she would need to gun it.

I lowered the jack, yanked it out of the way like a NASCAR pit crew and yelled, "Go!"

And Lisa gunned it. The horse trailer swayed crazily from side to side and her back truck tires flung mud all over the front of the trailer, but it was out of the ditch.

Lisa pulled into my yard, turned the trailer around and lowered the ramp, so we could load Aries right up. The problem now was getting him into the trailer.

We walked into the pasture and tried to get Aries to his feet. I remembered Matt saying that time was of the essence, and I could hear a clock ticking in my head.

I put his halter on and pulled, but to no avail. I tried smacking him and shoving on him the way Matt had that morning. He didn't move. Desperation filled me and that flicker was almost gone. Aries looked at me and heaved a mighty sigh.

And then Lisa looked at me with that look Matt had given me earlier and said, "Tammy ..."

And I turned my back to Aries. I looked at Lisa with tears in my eyes and I said, "No. Lisa, I'm not ready to give up on this horse."

And she didn't say, "You're being selfish" or "He's old" or "It's time to let go." Instead, she said, "If you're not ready, he's not ready. Let's try again."

"Ok," I said, my mind suddenly a bit clearer. "Well, this isn't the normal side he lies on. Shan and I flipped him onto this side. He usually lies on the left side. So maybe it will be easier for him to get up from his left side. Can you help me flip him back over?"

Of course, Lisa agreed to help, but after a couple of minutes straining and pulling, we still weren't able to flip him. So I asked Shannon to come help Lisa. She got one end of the lead rope and Lisa got the other. With the two of them pulling on one set of legs and me pulling on the other set, we finally managed to flip him to his left side.

And without hesitation, as soon as his left side hit the ground, Aries popped up on his feet. I quickly snapped my lead onto his halter and walked straight out of the pasture and onto the horse trailer. We were going to Auburn.

In my desire to get Aries on his feet, I hadn't noticed that I'd given Lisa the short lead rope, so she got clipped by Aries' hooves like I had earlier. But like any tough horse person, she shook it off quickly and was ready to drive. I insisted on riding in the trailer with Aries. Lisa knew it wouldn't do any good to argue with me, so away we went.

I was worried that Aries might try to lie down again on the way to Auburn. I wasn't sure how I planned to stop that, but I needn't have worried. Because once we flipped him the second time, he was fine. He was trembling with weakness and exertion, but his eyes were suddenly clear. I stroked and talked to him for the entire trip, and Lisa kept up with us via cell phone. Dr. Matt and Katie called to check in as well.

Matt had also called ahead to let Auburn know we were coming and there was an entire team of vets and students waiting for us. They examined Aries and let us know that his colon was indeed, back in place. Katie's "old cowboy trick" had worked. Thank God for cowboys and their tricks.

Aries spent the night at Auburn, just to make sure he was ok, and Katie took me to pick him up the next day. His crew at Auburn probably didn't get the chance to see too many 32-year-old horses, and they told me he was in impressive condition, and of course, they all told me how wonderful and beautiful he was. I was a lucky horse owner, indeed.

30 Sophie

ARIES was back home, healthy as a horse, but after seeing how he had reacted to the paint mare at Iron Gate, I knew I needed to find him a companion. I asked Lisa about buying Scarlett, but she wasn't for sale.

Also, I didn't exactly have the funds to buy another horse. My financial situation was getting better, but money was still in short supply. Lisa promised to keep an eye out for something for me.

So when Lisa called one day and said that she had a paint mare that needed a new home, I didn't even stop to think about it. "Bring her on," I said.

The mare was being boarded at Rock House, but the owners were moving to California. They'd been trying to sell her, but time was running short, so they said they'd just give her away if they could find someone who would give her a good home. Lisa heard about it and of course, thought of me.

Lisa brought the mare over and she was gorgeous – a buckskin paint. I only had electric fencing on my property, so I wanted to be there to keep an eye on her and also to make sure she and Aries were going to get along.

Lisa had brought a friend with her, so the four of us, Lisa, her friend, Shannon, and I all went into the pasture. I unhooked the fencing and let Lisa lead the mare in. Everyone else walked through, and I fastened the top strand back, like I always did when I went into the pasture.

Lisa introduced Sophie to Aries on the lead line, but all they did was sniff each other a bit and then they both dropped their heads and started grazing. No worries there, I thought.

So Lisa took the halter off and we all stood and watched them for a few minutes. However, as Sophie grazed closer and closer to the gate, I didn't realize she was eyeing the open gap under that top strand of wire until it was too late. She ducked her head, ran under the gate and down my driveway. Aries trotted down the fenceline and whinnied at her. "Come back!" he seemed to be saying. "You'll like it here. We have alfalfa! And apples!" But Sophie just kept going.

It was upsetting, but none of us were too concerned. I lived on a dirt road, so she wasn't going to run out into traffic or anything and she wouldn't get too far. A little feed in a bucket and we'd catch her, no problem.

When we got to the end of the road, however, my heart sank. The gate that was usually closed was open. And it opened up into that thousand-acre timber farm that Aries and I had roamed over for years. Lisa and I walked through the woods, shaking the feed bucket and calling her name. No sign of her. Not a glimpse, not a sound.

We called the Sheriff's Department and Animal Control and alerted them. If anyone reported a loose horse in the area, please call us. A stray horse isn't like a stray dog. Someone would see her. Someone would call.

Except that no one did. We walked the woods for hours, until it started getting dark and Lisa had to go take care of her family.

I went to bed, but couldn't sleep. I didn't even know the people who had owned Sophie, but they had trusted me to give her a good home. I'd given her a good home all right. For about five minutes. I thought about how I'd feel if that had been Aries. I'd have been furious. I'd have hated me. I did hate me.

The next day, and the day after that, and many days after that, I walked the trails and wandered around in the woods behind my house. I already knew a good bit about the property, but now I printed off Google Sky Maps, and plotted out search strategies. I typically walked for four hours at a time, accumulating blisters, sunburn, poison ivy, and ticks, but no horse. She had vanished into thin air.

I would equip myself with a halter and lead, a flashlight, my cell phone, and a walking stick that could double as a weapon in case I was attacked by coyotes. I never saw any coyotes, but I did see a lot of deer and turkey. But still no horse. For more than a month, I walked back there every day. I kept the feed bucket, halter and flashlight by my door and when I would hear noises in the woods at night or the dogs would start barking, I would think, "Maybe that's Sophie," and I would grab all that stuff and go off into the woods, calling for her in the dark.

When I told Joey I was doing that, he said, "Mom, it may not be a great idea to go *toward* the sounds in the woods in the middle of the night, with *feed in your hands.*"

He had a point. He was so worried about it, he made me promise not to do that anymore.

But one night, in the wee hours just before daylight, I heard my dogs bark. And I strained to listen and could hear something in the woods. I couldn't help myself. I stuffed my feet into my garden clogs and off I went into the dark. I walked down the trail in the direction I thought the noise was coming from. Another, smaller trail went off to the right, so I turned and went down that way for a while.

And then I saw a glimmer of lights. "What's that?" I thought. "Eyes shining in the dark?" Nope. It was headlights. It was a truck. And it was coming toward my house. I couldn't cross back over the trail without being caught in their headlights. I didn't know what to do. Hide behind some bushes? They would see me, and how ridiculous would that look? I was wearing hot pink pajamas for crying out loud. They'd probably already seen me.

So I straightened up, (I had instinctively squatted down when I realized what those mysterious lights were), and walked toward the main trail with as much nonchalance as I could muster.

The truck slowed down and then stopped. The first blush of dawn revealed a couple of hunters with ZZ Top beards and about eight teeth between the two of them.

I flashed them a big smile and said, "Good morning!" all cheery and bright, while the banjo music from *Deliverance* ran through my head, almost drowning out my heartbeat pounding in my ears.

"Mornin'," the driver said, leaning out the window. "Whatcha doin'?"

"Looking for a horse," I said, holding out the halter as proof that I wasn't doing anything crazy in the woods before sun-up in my hot pink pajamas and green garden clogs.

The passenger leaned forward, "That purdy white horse?"

"Oh no," I said. "Not that one. This one is a paint. She's brown and white. If you guys see her, or any sign of her, will you let me know?"

"Sure," said the driver. "You ok? You probably shouldn't be out here in the dark."

"I know," I said, "But I really need to find this horse. She's been gone for several weeks now."

"Is that white one ok?" the passenger asked.

Strangely, I found his concern for Aries touching, and again thought of how I'd feel if he'd been the one to disappear into the woods.

"He's ok," I said.

"Because he's been here a long time," he said.

"I know. He's thirty-two and I've had him since he was five." I didn't know why I volunteered that information, because I knew the follow-up question would be "How long do horses live?". But it wasn't.

"You must take real good care of him," the guy said, and suddenly I wanted to cry.

"You'll keep an eye out for me, won't you?" I asked again, "And let me know if you see anything at all. Hoof prints, manure, any sign at all."

"We will," the driver promised. "You'd best get inside before you catch your death of cold."

They drove off and I went back inside, but I was somehow comforted that they were looking out. If she was back there somewhere, they'd surely see some sign. And I knew they'd let me know. But I never heard from them. And no one ever heard from Sophie again either.

Personally, I think that someone found her and kept her. She was an exceptionally pretty mare, and I hope that wherever she ended up, whoever ended up with her, she is being taken great care of.

Eventually, after I gave up on finding Sophie, I tried other companions for Aries. Lisa brought me her pony Spot, but he didn't want to stay in my fence either.

And Michelle Wright brought me a pony named Starshine who stayed with us for several months, but she bullied Aries too much. At first it wasn't so bad, and I thought that after a while, she'd settle down and they'd get along the way Aries and Deb had. But after Starshine gave Aries a particularly nasty kick, I called Michelle and said it wasn't working out. She was happy because she'd kind of changed her mind and wanted the pony back anyway, but didn't know how to ask me.

And so it was back to just Aries and me.

31 THAT GOOD NIGHT

SOMETIME after Katie left home and was living in Virginia or Florida or California, she came home for a visit. She came to visit me, but she had also heard that a dear friend of hers had passed away, and she wanted to visit his wife to pay her condolences.

Dave and Iris lived near me, somewhere between my house and Rock House. It was at Rock House that Dave and Katie had become friends. Dave was an old-school cowboy, a horse trainer, a saddle maker, and a gentleman. His hand-made saddles were top notch and his training skills were in high demand. He taught Katie a lot and helped her iron out several problems with her horses. Katie probably had more respect for Dave than just about anybody in her life, and I was always grateful to anyone who helped out my daughter. I admired Dave as well, always feeling a bit like I was in the presence of John Wayne whenever he was around.

So we were both sad to hear of his passing, but Katie was more well-acquainted with his wife than I was. I went with her to see Iris, but mostly, I just murmured my condolences and then sat by, listening to Katie and Iris reminisce about Dave.

My heart ached for Iris as she talked about losing this extraordinary man. I longed to tell her how lucky she was to have had someone like that for as long as she did. But platitudes like that aren't much use to someone in pain, and I didn't know her that well. So I just sat and listened and nodded supportively.

Then she gazed out the window, into her front yard and said, "At least he won't have to bury that damn horse."

And I felt my heart rip in half. I couldn't see the horse in question from where I was sitting. I didn't know the horse's name, didn't know anything about it. But I knew from her tone that Dave had felt about "that damn horse" something like the way I felt about Aries. Shining through her sadness and a tinge of bitterness was genuine relief that the love of her life had been spared the pain of losing the horse he loved. It was the one silver lining.

But I knew that I probably wouldn't be allowed that particular silver lining.

* * *

Aries had always been fastidious about his stall. He refused to mess up in his stall unless he was confined for an extended period of time, preferring to wait instead until he was turned out in the pasture. When he was forced to poop in his stall, he always went in one corner. So while other horse owners would spend lots of time mucking out their horse's stall, I was typically in and out in mere minutes, and his shavings would stay pristine for a long time. Khan, on the other hand, was an extremely messy stall-keeper. He'd poop whenever and wherever the mood struck him, and then he'd pace back and forth constantly, grinding all that manure into the shavings. I hated cleaning his stall.

Aries was also particular about where he went in the pasture. There were no piles of manure lying willy-nilly wherever in my pasture. He had three distinct areas that he used, and perhaps coincidentally, they were all located behind a stand of trees or bushes. After Deb had been with us for a while, he too, conformed to the poop rules and rarely did I see a pile that wasn't in one of the designated areas.

Aries would, however, make an exception during thunderstorms, as he didn't like coming out of his stall into the rain.

That's how I first knew that Aries wasn't feeling well. It was summer and he was spending so much time in his stall, he didn't even care if he messed it up. I had to clean his stall twice a day, like most horse owners.

I didn't mind, and as always, just enjoyed his company, but I was worried. Plus, his breathing seemed to be more rapid and shallow.

Of course, I called Matt. He said he thought that Aries had developed anhidrosis, which meant that he couldn't sweat. So the summer heat was being particularly rough on him. Matt gave me medicine, and also told me that beer sometimes helped with anhidrosis.

So in addition to Aries' usual bag of apples at the grocery store, I started getting him a six-pack of beer. At first, I wasn't sure what kind to get. Was he an American Lager kind of guy? I didn't think so. As much as I'm sure he would admire the Budweiser Clydesdales, he was probably more of a craft beer kind of horse. Katie told me that Guinness worked best, but I tried several kinds, including apple ales. I added it to his feed every day, but sometimes also gave it to him straight from the bottle. He seemed to enjoy drinking the beer, but it didn't appear to help his breathing problem. Neither did the medicine Matt prescribed. And his rapid breathing had turned into wheezing and occasional coughing.

Aries seemed fine otherwise, though. His eyes were clear, his energy level was the same, he ate, he drank, he pooped, he scratched his head on my shoulder, and he did his ritual stretching routine. He was his normal self. It was easy for me to believe that this was a temporary problem, caused by heat or allergies, and as soon as it cooled off or the offending plants in his pasture died, he would be fine. If we had to move up north, so he didn't have to deal with the heat, I'd figure out how to do it. My sister lived in Colorado. Colorado would be good.

But then there were those telltale piles of manure in his stall.

I was on the phone with the vet's office constantly for about three weeks. Michelle Wright now worked there, and so it was nice to hear a familiar, sympathetic voice. After we'd tried giving him the medicine for anhidrosis, and his medicine for allergies, and he was still wheezing, I called to make another appointment with Matt.

But Matt didn't come. Instead, his partner Jason came. And Jason had a more grim diagnosis.

"I think he might have lung cancer," he said.

But I shook that possibility off, even though Aries had several melanomas that had been present for years. Grey horses often get melanomas, and they aren't usually a problem. I knew he had one inside his mouth and one inside one of his nostrils. I also knew that the one on his leg had recently grown, after being the same size for years. But I, like many people, am adept at burying my head in the sand. We would simply move to Colorado, buy a ranch, populate it pretty paint mares and super sturdy fencing and Aries would be fine.

And then one morning, I woke up to a strange sound. In my just-woke-up fugue, I didn't identify it for a few seconds. And then I realized it was Aries trying to breathe. And it was so loud I could hear it in my house.

Panicked, I jumped out of bed, and ran down to his stall. He was standing, head down, wheezing mightily, struggling to get air into his lungs. I had already dialed the vet's office before I got there. I left a tearful message and hung up.

I started to go into his stall, when he suddenly flung his head up and began staggering around. His eyes were wild and he was thrashing about. I stopped at his doorway, knowing if I went inside he could fall on me or pin me against a wall. He careened from side to side. He crashed into the divider between the stalls and a board cracked and splintered under his weight. I fell to my knees, overcome by my worst nightmare unfolding in front of me. Helpless to help him, all I could do was pray.

After a few long moments, he crashed to the floor of the stall and laid there, his sides heaving. Blood trickled out of his mouth and nostrils. I crawled inside his stall and used my shirt to wipe some of the blood away. I didn't want his face lying in the shavings like that, so I lifted his head and cradled it in my lap.

My phone rang. It was Jason. As soon as I said hello, he asked, "Is Aries down?"

"Yes," I replied.

"I'll be there as soon as I can," he said.

And that was that. I knew it was over. I called Shannon, who was still in the house.

When she answered, I said, "Please bring me apples."

"How many?" she asked.

"All of them," I said. "And please bring me another shirt."

After a few minutes, Shannon appeared, cradling an entire bowl of apples and dangling a t-shirt from her arm. She also brought a bottle of water for me. She handed it all over and then Shannon, who was fascinated by all things medical and who loved talking to the vet, simply left and went back into the house and did not come back out.

It was just Aries and me, his beautiful head still cradled in my lap. I offered him an apple, expecting him to ignore it, but to my surprise, he ate it. I almost laughed at my chow-hound of a friend. Nothing was going to keep him from eating apples, even if he had to do it lying down on his side, with his head in my lap. I fed him every single apple, and he seemed to start feeling better. He tried to get up, but only managed to get into the same lying position he usually slept in, with his legs folded underneath him. Still it was better than being stretched out on his side like that.

He wasn't wheezing anymore, and I began to think that maybe he was ok. Maybe it was a blood clot. He'd had a blood clot somewhere and it had burst and now it was gone and he was going to be okay. My desperate brain tried to come up with all kinds of possibilities to prevent that summer morning from ending the way I knew it was going to end.

When Jason arrived, Shannon directed him and his assistant down to the barn. I was sitting in the doorway of Aries' stall and he was still lying down, although his head was up and he was alert. When he saw the strangers approaching, he gave me a warning nicker. "Hey, you see there are people we don't know in my pasture, doncha?"

We got Aries to his feet and Jason did an examination, but I knew what his recommendation was going to be.

We led him out of his stall and up near the house, under the shade of a big tree. He paused near one of his designated poop areas, and I stopped and let him go. This was the cardinal sign of equine health, wasn't it? He could poop, so he must be ok. But I knew he wasn't, so on we went, moving as slowly as possible. Prolonging the inevitable.

Jason explained the procedure to me, and then asked if I wanted to stay with him. Of course, I *wanted* to stay with him. I thought of the dogs I had gone through this with, my arms wrapped around them until the end. But Aries wasn't a dog. He was a 1000 pound horse.

When Jason told me that he would just "go to sleep," I said, "But then he'll fall."

"But then he'll fall," Jason repeated.

I couldn't take that. I just couldn't watch. If I couldn't have my arms around him, I would rather say my goodbyes now.

And so I talked to him for a few minutes. Jason and his assistant stood nearby, just inside my peripheral vision. Stranger and almost-stranger witnessing the most painful moment of my life. Wrapped up in my own pain, it didn't occur to me that this must be the most difficult part of their job. Not the late night calls. Not the treks into overgrown pastures. Not the messy, smelly parts of the job. This.

I can't tell you exactly what I said as I murmured my goodbyes. I know I told him I loved him. That he was the most beautiful horse in the world (as if he didn't know). That I appreciated everything he had done for me and my family. That I believed with all my heart that I would see him again someday.

And no matter what anyone says or thinks, I know he understood.

32 GRIEF

IF Aries had been a person, I suppose there would have been flowers. And a procession of friends and relatives bearing casseroles, because I was from the South, after all. But because he was just a horse, there wasn't any of that. No flowers, no casseroles, no phone calls or visits to see how I was holding up. Not that I would have wanted any of that. I preferred to be alone with my grief. And I was definitely grieving.

I didn't want to talk to anyone about it. I didn't even talk to Katie about it. I sent her a text that simply said, "He's gone." It was two weeks before I could even post about it on Facebook. People responded with sympathy and kindness, because my friends are kind and sympathetic people. Katie's friend Shelley sent me a nice card in which she wrote that Aries and I "shared an epic bond." I liked that.

But nothing really eases grief but time. And even time isn't that great at it.

Unfortunately, I thought that perhaps vodka could do time's job, but do it more quickly.

I still went to work every day, and would arrive home in the wee hours of the morning. My eyes would still turn to the right as I drove down my driveway, still searching for that gorgeous white form in the darkness. As I got out of my truck, I would still pause, my ears listening for that familiar nickering. My feet still wanted to turn toward the garage, expecting to get a little nighttime snack of aromatic alfalfa to toss over the fence.

But there was nothing on the other side of that fence. My pasture was empty. So I would stand for a moment, and then go into the house and try to sleep. But as soon as my head hit the pillow, I would hear again that horrible wheezing sound. I would try to block it out, literally putting my hands over my ears, as if that would help. But it didn't.

So I would get up and get a drink. That didn't help either, but eventually, I would fall asleep. Or pass out, whichever. Sometimes, I would wake up in the pasture, lying on the freshly upturned earth that covered my best friend, the dirt damp and cool against my face. And I would go inside, shower, and go to work.

This must have gone on for at least two months, because I remember telling one of my bartenders that I thought I had drunk more alcohol in the past two months than in the rest of my life leading up to that point. And it was quite possibly true. I went through bottles of vodka like a marathon runner goes through Gatorade.

And because I did it in the night, in the solitude of my room, I thought Shannon didn't know. But Shannon knows more than anyone thinks she knows.

Sometimes, I would sit on my bed and drink straight from the bottle, and would simply pass out and sleep. Other times, sleep would still evade me. On those nights, I would question my decision to let him go. I would torture myself with "what ifs." What if I had taken him to Auburn one more time, what if I had moved us to Colorado, what if he had another 20 good years ahead of him, but I hadn't given him a chance? What if I had pulled the trigger too quickly, cheating him out of more time? Yeah, thirty-three was old, but there was that horse in England that was in his 50s...

And so one night, when I was going through this awful game of vodka-fueled "what if," I realized that I wasn't in my bedroom. I was standing in the middle of my living room. And Shannon was standing a few feet away from me. And she was saying something. No, she was asking something.

"Are you okay?"

I stood there quietly for a moment, staring at her bleary-eyed, swaying unsteadily on my feet. And then I screamed. I screamed at Shannon,

God help me. I screamed so loud and so hard that I felt every blood vessel in my body strain with the exertion.

"Am I okay?" I screamed. "No, I'm not okay! I KILLED MY BEST FRIEND!"

And then everything was completely quiet again. Without a word, Shannon turned and left the room, and I collapsed on the couch.

And then she came back. And she had a bottle of water, a cold washcloth, and a bottle of ibuprofen. She had my migraine kit. I'd suffered from debilitating migraines for years. And just as I could tell when Aries was colicking by looking at his face, Shan knew by looking at me when I had a migraine. She knew to keep the house quiet ... turn the TV down, turn the lights off ... and she would bring me those items. And eventually, I would get better. She was trying to make me better.

And so I poured out what little vodka I had left in the house and vowed not to buy any more. I had to stop feeling sorry for myself. What was done, was done. I had to stop blaming myself and focus on taking care of Shannon. And me.

But I didn't know what to do with myself. My whole life had been so wrapped up in Aries, my very identity centered around the fact that I owned the most beautiful horse in the world. I didn't feel like me without him. Also taking care of a horse is a bit demanding of your time, so suddenly, I had a lot of time on my hands. I decided I needed a hobby.

Gardening would be good, I thought. I could grow flowers. Flowers are beautiful. Not as beautiful as Aries, but pretty. Flowers are pretty. And I didn't think I would cry when the flowers died. So I tried planting flowers. Mums and tulips and hostas and camellias. And it's a good thing dead flowers didn't make me cry. Because I killed a lot of flowers.

It wasn't as if I didn't know what I was doing, although that was part of it. Because I'd never really tried to grow flowers. I had too many other things to do. But I knew how to read. So I knew that certain plants like sun and some like shade and some like wet soil and some like well-drained soil. I knew about deer and gophers and slugs. Because I knew how to read. But in practice, all I really wanted to do was plant them and then wait for them to come up and be pretty for me. They needed to grow and be pretty to pay me back for the work I'd invested, sticking them in the ground. They needed to be pretty and soothe my aching soul, dammit.

The flowers were, for the most part, uncooperative. And although I would continue to make half-hearted attempts at gardening, it wasn't what I needed to fill the void. Besides, the most beautiful flower in the world still wouldn't scratch its head on my shoulder.

So I decided I needed a dog. The only problem was that I already had five of them. Because the end of a dirt road apparently seems like a great place for people to dump their dogs off. So throughout the years, my little place in the middle of nowhere has been a stopping off point for dozens of dogs. I would find homes for most of them, making sure they were spayed or neutered first. At one point, I was taking so many dogs to a local low-cost spay and neuter clinic, that they started giving me the same discount they gave rescue organizations.

And although I did my best to take care of these dogs and give them a home, they didn't occupy the space in my heart that my other dogs had. They weren't Hooch, in other words. Or Trouble, Pixel, or Twinkie.

So what I needed, I thought, was another border collie. Border collies won't allow you to simply have them. They aren't a stay in the house or yard kind of dog and they don't tolerate an occasional pat on the head. They are workers and they demand that you give them something to do. You will pay attention to them. You will give them something to do. You will interact with them. Or they will destroy your house.

That, I thought, was exactly what I needed. But I didn't have time for a border collie at the moment. Still, it gave me something to think about.

One night, I was talking to my brother on the phone, and we were discussing books, as we often did. What he'd read, what I'd read, what we wanted to read. It's one of the things I really miss when the two of us go through our long periods of not speaking to each other. There's no one to give me good book recommendations.

And he said that someone had told him that he would like a book called *Eminent Dogs, Dangerous Men*. He hadn't read it yet himself, and didn't even know what it was about, but the title intrigued me, so as soon as I hung up the phone, I hopped on Amazon. I typed the title into the search bar, and found that the book in question had a subtitle. It was "Searching through Scotland for a Border Collie."

Huh, I thought. Well there's a coincidence. So of course, I ordered the book right away. It told the story of the author's search for a border collie to work on his sheep farm in Virginia. It also gave details about sheep herding competitions. I loved the book so much that I bought other books by the same author, Donald McCaig, and was most delighted when those books were about border collies.

Suddenly, I had something to dream about again. I would get some sheep, that's what I'd do. I'd have to convert my electric fence into something sturdier to keep sheep in. Maybe I could make money off the sheep. I knew myself well enough to realize that I probably wouldn't be able to sell them for meat, but maybe I could shear the wool and sell it. Maybe I'd buy a loom and weave the wool myself. I'd keep my own sheep, weave my own wool, have a border collie who'd love me, and we'd attend sheep herding competitions all over the world. And of course we'd win. And I'd be happy again. But not just yet.

Being a restaurant manager is much more demanding than most people realize. We work insane hours, on our feet, running around putting out fires ... sometimes literally. There was no time for me to train a border collie, much less get time off to travel to competitions. It wouldn't be fair to the dog for me to get him yet. But someday...

In the meantime, I'd found something else to occupy my time. A couple of my regulars at Smokey Bones had been doing genealogical research on their families, and they were traveling to other states to do research. They kept me up to date on their progress, and I found it very interesting.

So I got a membership on Ancestry.com and began poking around a bit. I thought that I'd be able to trace my father's family pretty easily, and that's what I'd intended in the beginning. I knew his family was supposed to be of German origin, and they were Quakers. So I thought that there would be easy paths to trace.

I didn't think I'd be able to trace my mom's family that easily, because she came from the Smokey Mountains in North Carolina and had a lot of Cherokee ancestors. But because there were so many redheads in our family, we also thought that we had Irish in us somewhere. My mom had the high cheekbones and long dark hair of a Cherokee, but she also had startlingly blue eyes that were inherited by Katie and Joey. But Katie was also one of the many redheads that continually popped up in the family.

Surprisingly, I hit a dead end with my father's family early on, and wasn't able to trace them very far. So I turned my attention to my mother's family and was rewarded with one line that stretched back to the Civil War and then even farther, across the sea to the British Isles. But not to Ireland, as I expected. No, my ancestors had come from Midlothian, an area around modern day Edinburgh. *Scotland*.

When I was a kid, I had a toy called a "Magic 8-ball." It was a black ball that looked like a billiards eight ball. It had a small window in one side and was filled with some kind of dark fluid. Inside the ball was a tiny white triangular shape. On this shape was printed responses to questions. You could ask your Magic 8 Ball anything. I suspect the question most often asked was, "Does Bobby love me?" (Or John or Billy or whoever). Then you'd shake the ball, turn it over with the window facing you, and that white triangle would swim up to the surface, with the answer to your question. Answers like "yes," "most certainly," or "my reply is no," and more ambiguous answers such as "reply hazy," "ask again later," and "signs point to yes."

Sitting at my computer, staring at proof that my family originated in Scotland, I remembered what the animal communicator had told me all those years before, about Aries and I knowing each other in another life. In Scotland.

And if I had a Magic 8 Ball and asked it what I needed to do to make myself happy again, I believe that little white triangle would have said, "All signs point to Scotland."

33 REDEMPTION

My insomnia worsened after losing Aries. When I would wake up, staring at the ceiling, I didn't know what to do any more. Years of grabbing a halter, apple, and flashlight and heading out into the pasture for a conversation with Aries were ingrained in me. I tried to go back to my old habit of writing in the middle of the night, but I had somehow lost that ability a couple of years before.

I had taken a nasty fall and had broken my leg and had a concussion. My recovery was long and painful, and I had lots of lingering effects. The most disturbing effects were cognitive. I would get confused. I would get lost on the way to work, after having traveled the same path for almost 20 years. Worst of all, I couldn't write. But I still had freelance clients, so I continued to try. But I started missing deadlines, which I had never done before. And I knew that the work I was turning in was sub-par. But I just couldn't figure out how to make it better. So the few freelance clients I had dwindled away until no one was left. Even FC&A had to stop giving me work. They said it was because they were no longer using freelancers, but I was sure it was because the quality of my work had gone downhill.

I left my job at Smokey Bones and took a manager position at Cracker Barrel. The training process at Cracker Barrel was intense and long. I was away from home for six weeks, and my brother came to stay with Shannon and look after her. No matter where my brother and I were in our relationship, he always loved Shannon and always tried to do what was best for her.

I still couldn't walk through the produce aisle at the grocery store, because the sight of apples or carrots made me choke up. I knew it was insane to still be feeling the way I did, but a line from "Mr. Bojangles," a song by the Nitty Gritty Dirt Band, kept running through my head.

The dog up and died. He up and died. And after twenty years he still grieves.

I wasn't drinking myself into oblivion, but I was still floundering. And I wondered if it was going to be that way for twenty more years.

Once again, life seemed bleak.

* * *

My oldest daughter is not a whimsical person. Practical, focused, driven … words like that are most often used to describe her. So when she asked me one day, "If you could go anywhere in the world, where would you go?" I should have known that it wasn't an idle question. But I didn't think about that. I simply answered, with no hesitation, "I'd go to Scotland to watch the Scottish National Sheepdog Trials."

And then I forgot about it.

Until a few months later, when Katie called to tell me that she and her husband were taking me with them on vacation again … this time to Scotland.

We would be flying into Edinburgh in May, so I wouldn't be able to see the sheepdog trials, which were held in August. Still, I was going to Scotland!

I began to plan our itinerary. I studied the Visit Scotland website and I subscribed to a photography page on Facebook called "Spectacular Scotland." I scoured AirBnB.com for the best family-friendly accommodations. I broke out Google Maps and plotted our courses, calculating drive times between destinations and gradually whittling down the overwhelming list of places I wanted to see into a busy, but manageable schedule. Finally, I had something I could work on during my bouts of insomnia. As much as I was looking forward to our trip, I was almost sad that my planning would come to an end. But everything was organized. Every detail taken care of.

Unfortunately, I didn't put quite as much thought and time into packing for the trip as I did into planning it. Suddenly, it was time to leave and I hadn't packed a thing. I ran around, throwing random stuff into a suitcase. As I was searching for something, (I can't remember what ... batteries for my camera maybe), I began frantically pulling open every drawer in the house. And I pulled open the drawer that contained Aries' grooming kit. A drawer I hadn't pulled open in the almost two years since he'd been gone. And there, lying in that drawer, was his mane comb. And in that mane comb was a mass of sparkling white strands of his mane. I stopped, my frantic efforts to pack forgotten. I stared at it for a moment, remembering how much I enjoyed combing out his mane ... how handsome he looked when I finished. For a moment, I considered my desire to clone Aries, but that thought was pushed aside almost immediately. I wasn't sure if it was technologically possible to clone from hair, but I was certain that, for me, it was financially impossible. And yet, I picked up the comb, pulled the hairs out, folded them into a neat, compact little bundle, and stuck them into my wallet. It was odd I know, but by God, I was taking Aries to Scotland with me.

I almost missed my flight, my suitcase was too heavy, and I was an obviously inexperienced traveler and terrible packer, but I was on my way. A TSA agent in London asked me where I was from, and when I told him Georgia, he asked me if I knew that "The Walking Dead" was filmed in Georgia. The show about zombies had taken over my little home town of Senoia, transforming it into a tourist attraction and one of the coolest new places to live. The thousand-acre timber farm where I rode Aries for years, where I once lost a horse and had trudged through pretty much every inch looking for her, had been sold to a developer and soon they would pave my road and build five hundred houses behind my little five acre patch of dirt. My middle of nowhere was suddenly the middle of somewhere and I didn't like it. But as the agent passed the wand around my shoulders and under my armpits, I politely told him that yes, I was aware. And I wasn't going to worry about that now, because I was almost in Scotland.

The first few days, we stayed in Edinburgh, which is built on seven hills, like Rome. Edinburgh Castle is built on Castle Rock, part of an extinct volcano. In other words, Edinburgh is very hilly, with lots of steps everywhere. Since I wasn't a spring chicken anymore, and my daughter and her husband were both athletes who had no trouble at all hiking up hills and climbing steps, I definitely slowed everyone down. But they indulged me.

Our first stop was Edinburgh Castle. The most interesting part of Edinburgh Castle for me was the tiny little graveyard where the soldiers supposedly buried their dogs. I mean seriously, who cares about Crown Jewels, when you can see dog graves?

After that my family further indulged my eccentricity as we went on a quest to find a specific dog that had been dead for over 130 years. Greyfriar's Bobby was a Skye terrier that spent 14 years guarding his master's grave at Greyfriar's Kirk. He become sort of famous, someone wrote a book about him, someone built a statue of him. Of course I had to see the statue and his grave. We wandered through miles of Edinburgh hills before we found it, mere moments before they locked the kirkyard gates. I have the absolute best family.

We saw the Kelpies, which were located in Falkirk, just a few miles away from Edinburgh. The Kelpies are the largest equine sculptures in the world. Two horse heads, built from interlocking steel beams, tower over the surrounding landscape. The name was derived from the mythical kelpies, transforming creatures who could turn themselves into horses, lure someone onto their backs and then plunge into the water with their prey, drown them, and eat them. The statues were built as an homage to the working horses of Scotland, and in fact, two real Clydesdales were used as models. Clydesdales, like border collies, originated in Scotland.

After a few days in Edinburgh, we traveled to the northern end of the island, to Gordon Castle, to watch the first Highland Games of the season. It was a glorious day. Manly men in kilts heaved heavy things into the air, there were lots of activities for my granddaughter, and of course, there were dogs. Border collies, Scottie dogs, greyhounds, German shepherds, dogs of every description. And every one of them was perfectly socialized and well-behaved.

We visited some standing stones, at Clava Cairn, near Inverness, and then we drove to our bed and breakfast to spend the night before going on to the Isle of Skye the next day.

I had booked this particular B&B because, besides being perfectly located on Loch Ness, and a great stopping point before heading onto the Isle of Skye the next day, it was family-friendly. As I had searched for accommodations, finding one that was family-friendly had proved a bit difficult. Of course, we could have stayed at a Holiday Inn, but who wants to do that when you're in Scotland?

The B&B was located near the town of Drumnadrochit, near the Loch Ness Centre and Exhibition. On its website, there was a photo of shaggy-haired Highland Cattle, and it promised that children would enjoy petting the animals. It seemed perfect.

When we arrived, we went into a small reception area that appeared to double as a laundry room. We rang the bell and as we waited, I noticed a photo on the wall. A woman sat on a grey horse in hunter show attire.

"Is that an Arabian?" I asked Katie.

She glanced at it and said, "Maybe. Could be a Welsh. There's probably lots of them around here."

The owner came out and showed us to our rooms. My granddaughter was delighted to find that they supplied lots of toys for children ... bicycles and scooters, even a trampoline. Best of all, there were two adorable lambs in a stall just across from our accommodations. The owner let my granddaughter help feed them from bottles.

In a paddock nearby, I could see a couple of the Highland cattle from the photos on the website, and also a couple of horses ... one of them a grey that could possibly be the one in the picture I'd seen.

The setting was gorgeous, the weather was perfect, my granddaughter was having fun ... it was amazing. We got a taxi into town and had dinner in a restaurant overlooking Loch Ness. We had a charming redheaded Scottish waiter who apparently didn't know anything about wine, and simply gathered up a variety of bottles in his arms and carried them all to our table so we could choose.

We had a lovely evening and then went to bed, planning on getting up relatively early to continue our journey to the Isle of Skye.

We were in the family suite, which had one large bedroom and then a smaller one with twin beds. My granddaughter and I slept in the smaller room. This room was situated quite close to the horses' stalls.

And one of the horses had a cough.

I was worn out from all the traveling and fun we'd had and sleepy from the wine, and so I fell asleep rather quickly. But I didn't sleep well. Because every time the horse would cough, it would trigger a dream. I would dream of that terrible day when I lost my best friend. But slowly, the dream would cease to be disturbing, and instead would transition into Aries and I simply hanging out, riding the trails behind my house or along the shores of Loch Ness. Then the horse would cough again, and the dream would turn distressing again. And then soothing and positive. And then a cough and back again. On and on all night, I dreamed of Aries, good scenarios and bad ones.

And when I finally woke in the morning, I felt so strange. Incredibly agitated and yet serene at the same time. As if my alternating dreams had been rolled up into one big ball in my stomach. I rose and dressed while everyone else was still asleep and stepped outside.

The horses had already been fed and turned out in their paddocks. The morning was cool and misty, and as I gazed at the mountains with clouds shrouding their peaks, I suddenly realized why Scottish Highlanders would have been drawn to settle in the Smokey Mountains of North Carolina. The two places were almost interchangeable in look and feel.

On an impulse, I turned and went back inside, carefully shutting the door so as not to wake anyone. I opened my wallet and pulled out the small white bundle of Aries' mane and stuck it in my pocket. I walked down to the paddock, next to where the horses were grazing. Neither of them were coughing in the cool morning air. I stood for a few moments, taking in the beautiful view, the serenity of it all. And I pulled out that tiny white bundle that was all I had left of Aries, and I dropped it to the ground.

I stayed there a few minutes longer and I walked away, feeling as if I'd left Aries in the best place that I could. And I felt an inexplicable and enormous sense of release.

When I went to settle up the bill before breakfast, the owner took me upstairs to their home, chatting amiably. And I had to take the opportunity to ask.

"The horse in the picture downstairs," I said, "Is it an Arabian?"

"Yes!" he answered, beaming at me. "That's my wife's horse, the grey one in the paddock. She was horse of the year in England twice."

How I had managed to choose a bed and breakfast in the middle of Scotland that was home to a beautiful and adored grey Arabian, I don't know. But I chose to think that something had guided me there. Something that wanted me to be happy.

When I arrived home in Atlanta, I felt like a different person than the one who'd left a week before. Not just invigorated from the vacation. It had in fact, been a rather exhausting vacation. But something was definitely different. Something I'd have to mull over and consider. Analyze it ... because that's what I do.

When I posted about Aries' passing on my Facebook page, I mentioned the concept of the "Rainbow Bridge" and said that I hoped that it was true ... that all the animals you've loved in your lifetime would come running to meet you. If so, I'll have a veritable stampede awaiting me.

I've always been a bit shaky in my "beliefs." It comes from having an open mind. As I've said, I don't disbelieve much of anything. And I've always been open to consider another person's point of view. Some people would say that makes me wishy-washy. Decide what you believe and stick to it, already. But finally, I knew what I believed. And I realized that, despite my fervent promise to Aries almost two years before, I wasn't sure. I didn't really *believe it*. But now I do. I believe that I will see Aries again, and the sense of peace that came from that was immeasurable.

Aries had been my driving force for most of my life and had given me so many gifts. He enticed me out of my socially-inept shell. He inspired me to lose weight. He motivated me to go back to school. He helped my oldest daughter begin a career. As a lesson horse, he helped my family financially. He was the reason I bought my house in the middle of nowhere. He was the reason I clung to it with such tenacity. He was my anchor and my best friend for almost thirty years. And now that I had returned from my trip to Scotland, I realized that he had given me the best gift of all. Wonderful memories and stories. I thought I had lost my ability to write, but somehow, I had to share Aries' story. I had to tell people how amazing he was. How much he meant to me. One last time, Aries was going to be my motivation.

I sat down at my computer and I started to write.

73868545R00131

Made in the USA
Columbia, SC
19 July 2017